INHUMAN NATURE

INHUMAN NATURE

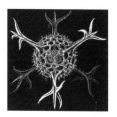

edited by Jeffrey Jerome Cohen

Oliphaunt Books | Washington, DC

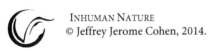

INHUMAN NATURE
© Jeffrey Jerome Cohen, 2014.

First published in 2014 by
Oliphaunt Books
Washington, DC
http://www.oliphauntbooks.com/

an imprint of punctum books
Brooklyn, New York
http://punctumbooks.com

Oliphaunt is sponsored by the George Washington University Medieval and Early Modern Studies Institute. Our mission is to create and sustain lively scholarly conversations on topics of wide interest across time periods and disciplines so that traditional methods for understanding historical and literary texts meet innovative modes of analysis, argumentation, and publication.

ISBN-13: 978-0692299302
ISBN-10: 0692299300

Cover Image: from Ernst Haeckl, *Kunstformen der Natur* (1904), Plate 96: Chaetopoda.

TABLE OF CONTENTS

Introduction: Ecostitial
Jeffrey Jerome Cohen
// i

Shipwreck
Steve Mentz
// 1

Hewn
Anne F. Harris
// 17

Human
Alan Montroso
// 39

Matter
Valerie Allen
//61

Recreation
Lowell Duckert
// 79

Trees
Alfred Kentigern Siewers
// 101

Fluid
James Smith
// 115

Inhuman
Ian Bogost
// 133

Acknowledgments

Inhuman Nature, the third title published by Oliphaunt Books in partnership with punctum books, would not have been possible without the unflagging support of Eileen Joy. A participant on the panels from which this book derives as well as the driving force behind punctum and a longtime forger of new worlds for humanities research, Eileen has both my abiding gratitude and admiration. Oliphaunt is sponsored by the George Washington University Medieval and Early Modern Studies Institute (GW MEMSI), a scholarly center funded by a collaboration between the GW Office of the Vice President for Research, the Office of the Provost, and the Columbian College of Arts and Sciences. I thank Leo Chalupa, Forrest Maltzman, and Ben Vinson III for their faith in us. I am also grateful to the twenty faculty members in nine departments who belong to the center for making it all work, somehow.

This book had its genesis in "Ecologies of the Inhuman," a roundtable at the International Congress of Medieval Studies in Kalamazoo, Michigan in May 2012. The event generated so much lively conversation that we reconstituted the gathering several months later in Washington, DC, under the auspices of GW MEMSI. Ian Bogost joined us for that second event and astonished us with his passion for Marie de France . . . and his willingness to embrace this group of medievalists and early modernists interested in what happens when ecology is framed non-anthropocentrically. Carolyn Dinshaw participated in both the roundtable and the MEMSI symposium, and I thank her for her engagement. Creative presentations, camaraderie, and some late nights at the Venetian Room of the Hotel Lombardy in DC ensured a shared sense of endeavor that culminated in this book.

Haylie Swenson ensured that every detail of the event came together.

I am grateful to the contributors to this volume for their talent, their perseverance, and their brilliance. I cannot imagine a better group with which to work.

INTRODUCTION:
ECOSTITIAL

Jeffrey Jerome Cohen[1]

Inhuman Nature maps the activity of the things, objects, forces, elements, and relations that enable, sustain and operate indifferently to the category and creature *human* (with "in-" functioning simultaneously as negative prefix and inclusive preposition, surfacing entanglement even at moments of abjection). *Nature* signifies both the qualities of these inhuman activities and relations, as well as ecological enmeshment. *Inhuman* is full of affect (a word for cruelty and barbarity, humane feelings' failure) as well as a neutral designation for excesses of scale (too vast or miniscule for familiarity); a separation within incorporation; negation belied by production; an antonym that fails. *Nature* is the great outdoors as well as a disposition towards kindliness (derived

[1] I thank the contributors for their provocative thinking, excellent writing, and enduring conviviality. The brilliant Anne Harris gave me the title for this introduction and helped me to think through its theme.

from *kynde*, the Middle English word that French *nature* replaced), hostility (crimson teeth and claws), or indifference (the universe that is not for us, where we are specks and milliseconds). That's a great deal of work with which to burden two words. Yet *inhuman* and *nature* together convey the shared endeavor of this book, not because they are precise, but because in their coupling they foreground the difficulties of speaking of that which is not us within narratives we fashion. Yet story making, scientific or artistic, would not be possible without a great many inhuman allies—and language acts upon its users as much as speakers and writers employ language. Few things in this world remain compliant long. Although their agency is not necessarily easy to behold, without a networked alliance of nonhumans you would not be reading these words, nor could I sit at my laptop, typing an introduction to a collection of essays on that very topic while a summer storm dashes rain and bamboo leaves against the window.

Enamored by fictions of environmental sovereignty, we imagine ourselves solitary. Our writing and our thinking habitually disregard the mediations of syntax and style, the pushback from pen or keyboard, the agency that flows within a fondness for dark coffee, the musing to which thunderstorms are intimate as triggers and intensifiers. Auguste Rodin's iconic bronze sculpture *Le Penseur* [*The Thinker*] seems an entire world: a body stripped bare and arched into a self-contained emblem for Philosophy, a human figure curved almost into the globe itself. Its muscular autonomy suggests the inward vectors of contemplation, the privacy of cognition—as well as their unthought gendering (Rodin's *Thinker* offers an ostentatiously male body). But what of that which supports philosophy's introspection, the boulder that affords foundation?[2] Without the stone (sometimes fashioned of bronze, sometimes of granite), the numerous castings of this statue would lack support, would tumble into indignity. What if instead of curving into anthropocentric selves we extend apprehension outward into the ecomateriality with which we are palpably embroiled, plumbing that which undergirds knowledge and abides in quiet affinity to all processes of knowing?[3] What if we attended to the "potent ethi-

[2] Michel Serres asks a similar question of the rock that accompanies Sisyphus into mythic time in *Statues: Le second livre des fondations* (Paris: Éditions François Bourin, 1987).
[3] On ecomateriality as a spur to thinking ecological networks see the

cal and political possibilities" evident in the enmeshment of the human body with "more-than-human nature," in what Stacy Alaimo so well labels trans-corporeality?[4] Stone, for example, enables movement and violence, extends cognition, and invites world-building. Calculus, the study that makes possible chemistry and engineering, is a Latin word that means "small stone," a counter that glides along an abacus, the means by which we outsource our reckonings to pebbles and string. "Calculus" is in turn intimately related to the support of body and dwelling, to calcium—the mineral that enables flesh to swim, to fly, to run. This same substance under subterranean pressure yields limestone and marble, matter for courts and temples. Always supported by objects, substances, and ecologies, the human is never uncompanioned.

Primal, enduring, and intractable, the lithic in philosophy typically stands in for nature itself: the given, the really real, a trope for the inhuman. When the nature for which it offers an emblem marks utter difference from the human, stone arrives into thought limned by terror. Seeking an endurance not ours, we fashion headstones from granite to remember the dead, incise glorious achievements into bright marble, stories stamped on lifeless things. These lithic structures offer not lasting memorialization but future oblivion, "colossal wreck, boundless and bare." All things fall to ruin, all things betray our desire to persist, all things enjoin the mighty to despair. To be human is to inhabit a world in which our burden is self-awareness. Blank stone becomes a metaphor for ruination, for nature's disregard. Barbara Hurd's *Entering Stone: On Caves and Feeling through the Dark* therefore begins her exploration of the substance with a moment of subterranean panic.[5] Crawling through a narrow limestone cave, deep within the ground, she feels the

special issue of the journal *postmedieval* on "Ecomaterialism," edited by Lowell Duckert and myself (Issue 4.1: 2013).

[4] Stacy Alaimo, *Bodily Natures: Science, Environment, and the Material Self* (Bloomington: Indiana University Press, 2010), 2. Alaimo defines trans-corporeality as the ways in which "the human is always intermeshed with the more-than-human world," underlining "the extent to which the substance of the human is ultimately inseparable from the environment" (2). See also her essential discussion of material agency and worldly emergence (143).

[5] Barbara Hurd, *Entering Stone: On Caves and Feeling through the Dark* (Boston: Houghton Mifflin, 2003).

world's weight impinge. She fears she will be crushed—by the world's palpable weight, by the dislodging of her own pasts, "what lingers unseen . . . a myriad of other selves inside me wakened from deep slumber."[6] These long-interred and affect-laden fragments of biography threaten to dissolve her, just as the cavern's petric substance was dislodged by water to form networks of narrow tunnels. Christine Marsden Gillis likewise uses stone to plumb autobiography, discerning in its density and separateness a bleak promise. She writes of a cemetery on a small island in Maine where she has buried her young son: "we were leaving that trace, not to shift with wind and tide on a sandy beach, but to endure in hard ground and rock."[7] Gillis's story attempts to petrify remembrance by attaching names and histories to lithic security. Gotts Island, "a place of stone remnants" and ruined houses, becomes an eternal memorial, its vitality evident in ephemera like wildflowers, frost, storms. The granite that forms the island's substance and keeps it anchored against temporal whirl is lifeless, transfixing human stories by removing them from the stream of time. Except, of course, cliffs erode, foundations tumble, gravestones crack when frost invades their pores. Names and dates fade. Particular histories recede.

Rock conveys perilous knowledge. Gillis and Hurd's "geobiographies" discover in inhuman nature an emotion-rich trigger to narrative. Yet because they separate this nature from the human, they do not plumb the ecologies upon which and through their narratives are built. As Stacy Alaimo's trans-corporeality or what Laura Ogden describes as material entanglement make clear, segregation of human and inhuman, nature and culture belies a complicated reality, an intertwined environmentality.[8] Inhuman forces and objects ultimately refuse domestication, refuse reduction into familiar tales as ancillaries and props (even as they domesticate—*ecologize*—themselves, each other, us). They in-

---

[6] Hurd, *Entering Stone*, 71–72.

[7] Christina Marsden Gillis, *Writing on Stone: Scenes from a Maine Island Life* (Lebanon: University Press of New England, 2008), 20.

[8] "Landscapes are assemblages constituted by humans and nonhumans, material and semiotic processes, histories both real and partially remembered": Laura Ogden, *Swamplife: People, Gators, and Mangroves Entangled in the Everglades* (Minneapolis: University of Minnesota Press, 2011), 35. Visions of "pure nature," she writes, are inevitably the "selective vision of empire" (71) that sees in landscape a space for domination.

tensify, enable, transmute, and resist, exerting agency, per-
turbing that frail border erected to keep the social from the
natural. Keen boundaries become on closer examination
messy interstices, environmental meshes, "ecostices." Bruno
Latour has argued cogently against what he calls the Great
Bifurcation, the division of culture from nature:

> a virus never appears without its virologists, a pulsar
> without its radioastronomers, a drug addict without his
> drugs, a lion without his Masai, a worker without her un-
> ion, a proprietor without her property, a farmer without
> landscape, an ecosystem without its ecologist, a fetishist
> without his fetishes, a saint without her apparitions.[9]

Rapturous in its incongruities, this catalog of human and
nonhuman alliance enacts a lexical, cognitive, and affective
commingling. Proliferative and sonorous, disinhibiting reduction back into constitutive elements, the litany performs
the very tangle it propounds, radiating aesthetic force. Although he worries that Latour's actor network theory dispers-
es objects across networks at the expense of their own integrity, Graham Harman has similarly attempted a "vigorous
means of engagement" that would "replace the piously over-
valued 'critical thinking' with a seldom-used *hyperbolic* thinking"[10] Insisting that humans are merely some actors among
many, none of which are exceptional or *a priori* privileged,
Harman's hyperbolic thinking is not all that different from
what medieval romance calls *aventure*, the marvelously disruptive emergence (*avenir*) of nonhuman agency, disclosed
when ordinary objects like rings, gems, swords, bottles of
fluids demonstrate their power to disrupt, waylay, and en-
chant.
   When Harman writes in a romance mode that "phenomenology must also include the description of nonexistent
objects, given that centaurs and unicorns can appear before
my mind no less than masses of genuine granite," he grants
matter in the form of the lithic an undeniable solidity, a
bluntness that imaginary creatures cannot hold even when

---

[9] Bruno Latour, *Politics of Nature: How to Bring the Sciences into
Democracy*, trans. Catherine Porter (Cambridge: Harvard University
Press, 2004), 165–166.
[10] Graham Harman, *Prince of Networks: Bruno Latour and Metaphysics* (Melbourne: re.press, 2009), 120.

they exert a certain agency.[11] Harman's essay on literary criticism "The Well-Wrought Broken Hammer" is built around the first tool adopted by human beings, a nexus of human and inhuman that functions as cultural origin point. Knapped from flint and used as weapon and tool, the hammer was humanity's first technological ally, the product of our first reaching towards something more durable than flesh. This transformative association between lithic tools and the primeval is medieval as well as modern. In Wace's *Roman de Brut,* a history of Britain, the aboriginal giants who dwell on the island attack its first human settlers "od pierres, od tinels, od pels" ("with stones, clubs, and stakes"), while the settlers meanwhile drive away their attackers with more technologically advanced but nonetheless functionally similar metals: "od darz, od lances, od espees / E od saetes barbelees" ("with spears, lances, swords, and barbed arrows").[12] That any tool can transmute or fail points to the ways in which an object will always exceed both use-value and human comprehension. When we grant a material like stone the dignity of its proper duration, moreover, we discern that this inert and natural substance is forever in motion, even though our own lives are too swift to perceive its restless transits. Philosophy's stone, that object upon which the Thinker sits in order to ruminate, that thing unthought so that thinking can proceed, that chunk of the real that stands for inhuman nature, actually resembles what medieval writers called the Philosopher's Stone, *lapis philosophorum.* The alchemical agent by which dull lead attains gold's radiance, the philosopher's stone is the *al-iksir* or elixir or undefinable substance through which mortal bodies obtain a geological duration, that "privee stoon" (secret rock) that withdraws from knowledge even as it precipitates movement, creativity, frustration, explosion, and exploration without end.[13]

[11] Graham Harman, "The Well-Wrought Broken Hammer: Object-Oriented Literary Criticism," *New Literary History* 43 (2012): 186 [183–203].

[12] Wace, *Roman de Brut: A History of the British,* ed. and trans. Judith Weiss (Exeter: University of Exeter Press, 2003). Quotations at 1091 and 1097–1098.

[13] "Privee stone" is Chaucer's description of the infinitely deferred philosopher's stone in the "Canon Yeoman's Tale" (at 1452): *The Riverside Chaucer,* gen. ed. Larry D. Benson, 3rd edn. (Boston: Houghton Mifflin, 1987). Gower speaks of the "philosophres ston" and its relation to alchemical learning in the *Confessio Amantis* 4.2523: John Gower, *Confessio Amantis, Volume 1,* ed. Russell A.

A similarly disjunctive yet lyrical series of objects opens Jane Bennett's *Vibrant Matter*, in which a collection of refuse on a Baltimore storm drain becomes a catalogue poem and a call to witness matter's radiance. Bennett heightens the vivid particularity of each object in the accidental assemblage: "one large men's plastic work glove one dense mat of oak pollen one unblemished dead rat one white plastic bottle cap one smooth stick of wood."[14] Collecting in astonishing distinctiveness "the countless things that litter our world unseen," this litany of detritus clinging to a grate could offer a dark ecology, the task of which is "to love the disgusting, inert and meaningless."[15] Yet, there is nothing repellent or still in Bennett's debris. The vignette renders the dross of the world alluring, lively, saturated with significance—a poetics of re-enchantment, the becoming-lyrical of matter.[16] This surplus inheres within the nature of worldedness itself. Manuel De Landa describes posthuman nature as "a positive, even joyful conception of reality."[17] It is also passionate, lyrical, alluring. Within the enmeshments necessary for anything to happen, humans and inhumans intermingle to create hybrid forms and collaborative agencies. Inhuman nature is irreducibly complicated because it is unfinished, nonprogressive, dispersed across multiple action-makers and materializers.

Self-appointed sovereigns of inhuman nature, we are used to placing our demands casually upon these environments. We seldom think about what nonhumans might desire for themselves. In *Aramis, or the Love of Technology*, Bruno Latour composes a novelistic account of inhuman

---

Peck, with Latin translations by Andrew Galloway (Kalamazoo: Medieval Institute Publications, 2000); http://www.lib.rochester.edu/camelot/teams/-rpca1int.htm.

[14] Jane Bennett, *Vibrant Matter: A Political Ecology of Things* (Durham: Duke University Press, 2010), 4.

[15] The first quotation is from Ian Bogost's excellent account of the workings of the nonhuman in *Alien Phenomenology, or What It's Like to Be a Thing* (Minneapolis: University of Minnesota Press, 2012), 51. For dark ecology see Timothy Morton, *Ecology Without Nature: Rethinking Environmental Aesthetics* (Cambridge: Harvard University Press, 2009), 195.

[16] I've written about this power in "An Abecedarium for the Elements," *postmedieval: a journal of medieval cultural studies* 2.3 (2011): 291–303.

[17] Manuel De Landa, *A Thousand Years of Nonlinear History* (New York: Serve Editions, 2000) 274.

desire in action.[18] Through a genre he dubs "scientifiction," he traces why a personal rapid transport system envisioned for Paris failed. Through multiple voices (some imagined, some the transcripts of actual interviews), the book's protagonist pieces together the reasons for the foundering of Aramis, as the system was poetically christened. With an emphasis upon the negotiations and subsequent transformations that convey ideas into materiality, Latour details the shifting alliances among human and inhuman actors, arguing that adaptation-demanding movements rather than technological limitations triggered the project's abandonment. Meshworks of living beings, organizations, materials, ideas, beliefs, forces and objects constitute both the social and the natural, neither of which possess inherent explanatory force. The task of the investigator is to trace weak and strong confederations, to examine whether something is well or poorly constructed, rather than to pull back a curtain and demystify origin: causality is not located in pre-existent social formations, but is glimpsed from the perspective of the things themselves in how they work, ally, or fail. Latour's emphasis on composition over critique demands an accounting for nonhuman agency. Partway through the book the unrealized personal transport system itself begins to speak, accusing its imaginers of lacking love sufficient to sustain its coming into being. In his bitter reproach, Aramis compares himself to Victor Frankenstein's spurned Creature, culminating his accusation with: "Burdened with my prostheses, hated, abandoned, innocent, accused, a filthy beast, a thing full of men, men full of things, I lie before you. Eloï, eloï, Lama, lama sabachthani" (158). Not exactly subtle, but his point is clear: when agency works through enmeshment, responsibility and desire (indistinguishable from movement, from life) are not the province of humans alone.

Latour's *Politics of Nature* contains a similarly ecstatic moment in which a careful explication of how collectives are formed swerves into fairy tale, invoking a magical figure from Sleeping Beauty:

Let us not forget the fairy Carabosse! On the pile of gifts offered by her sisters, she put down a little casket marked *Calculemus!* But she did not specify *who* was supposed to calculate. It was thought that the best of all possible

---

[18] Bruno Latour, *Aramis, or the Love of Technology*, trans. Catherine Porter (Cambridge: Harvard University Press, 1996).

worlds was calculable . . . . Now, neither God nor man nor nature forms at the outset the sovereign capable of carrying out this calculation. The requisite "we" has to be produced out of whole cloth. No fairy has told us how. It is up to us to find out. (164)

To calculate, used here to denote the adding of sums that refuse to cohere, returns us to *calculus*, the rock that enables cognition and culture, the trigger to thinking and doing, the inhuman nature upon which *Le Penseur* rests. Taken for granite: only when the passivity of inhuman nature is presumed do its abiding alliances become difficult to discern. The power of objects to disrupt human endeavors by refusing to be reduced to tidy equations and known-in-advance formulae hinges upon a small stone. How much more power, then, must an entire ecology of the inhuman hold: a summons to shared space, to an embroiled expanse beyond easy partition.

I completed this introduction in the woods of a small mountain in West Virginia, not far from the New River Gorge. Working over the draft, I was accompanied and sustained by still weather, birds sending messages through dense foliage, the flutter of flies and moths. At night I built a fire that crackled and listened to distant storms. Some of what I wrote derived from the usual agony of seeking the right word and clarifying ideas intent to elude, while other portions arrived fully formed and to my surprise. A good IPA, coffee, cheese, cherries and a responsive laptop fueled some of the thinking. The ideas of this book's contributors and the imagined arrival of the volume into your own hands also propelled me. I was never alone.

SHIPWRECK

Steve Mentz

Living inside shipwreck: it's what we're doing, admit it or not. One task of art and criticism is teaching us how best to admit it. Even, perhaps, to love it.

Three artistic near-disasters, which are also stories about disaster—James Cameron's film *Titanic* (1997), Bob Dylan's song "Tempest" (2012), and Thomas Pynchon's novel *Inherent Vice* (2009)—help the process. All three works are flagrent, over-the-top melodramas. Aesthetic disasters, they flout acceptable artistic standards: 194 minutes and $200 million dollars of cinematic schmaltz? a fourteen-minute talkin' waltz about the "Titanic" on a rock album? a goofy detective novel with a hippie-stoner Private Eye hero? In courting disaster, these three works imagine what it's like living inside disaster. Shipwreck ecology comes out the other end.

Making sense of the surging tides of shipwreck ecology starts with a line I've quoted before, one of my favorites, from the philosopher Michel Serres.[1] He writes about mari-

---

[1] I quoted this previously in the conclusion to "Strange Weather in

time disaster near the end of *The Natural Contract*: "I live in shipwreck alert. Always in dire straits, untied, lying to, ready to founder" (124). I liked this sentiment in 2010 when I first quoted it, and I like it still, but lately it's been bugging me. It's almost right, but not quite. It names my very deed of love for our inhuman environment but, as Lear's middle daughter might say, it comes too short.[2] Another Serres text, *The Five Senses*, imagines the experience of shipwreck as the birth of the soul.[3] Shipwreck ecology seems closer to birth than alert.

This essay follows Serres's metaphors of alert and birth while also extending both into an ecological vision of shipwrecked immersion in the company of Cameron, Dylan, and Pynchon. Shipwreck isn't something to prepare for, something that's about to happen. It's happening. Now. We're inside it, not waiting for it.

The thing is, it's not so bad inside shipwreck. It doesn't require us to howl in pain, though shipwreck provides fewer dry beds and calm nights than we might wish. The whole process becomes easier if you stop hoping that there is solid ground somewhere. This, by the way, is where I part ways with Lucretius and the "shipwreck with spectator" philosophical bank-shot tradition that uses visible disorder to solidify higher intellectual order.[4] I don't think we ever reach solid ground, no matter how hard we try. My point is that shipwreck—by which I mean the sudden shocking awareness that the mighty vessels that have carried us this far are coming to pieces under our feet—represents a perfectly ordinary way to live. My stalking horse in thinking about catastrophe is global warming, of course, but the underlying facts of disruption and disorder precede the Anthropocene.[5] Hu-

---

King Lear," Shakespeare 6.2 (2010): 147.

[2] See *King Lear*, 1.1.69–76. Cited from *The Riverside Shakespeare*, 2nd edn., ed. G. Blakemore Evans (Boston: Houghton Mifflin, 1997). All further quotations from Shakespeare from this edition cited parenthetically in the text.

[3] Michel Serres, *The Five Senses: A Philosophy of Mingled Bodies (I)*, trans. Margaret Sankey and Peter Cowley (London: Continuum, 2008), 17–21. I thank Jeffrey Cohen for this reference.

[4] On this tradition, see Steve Mentz, *At the Bottom of Shakespeare's Ocean* (London: Continuum, 2009), 19–32.

[5] I don't in the least doubt the science of anthropic climate change, but I have some concerns about the anthropocentrism of the term

mans have been floundering about inside disorder for a long time.

We've gotten good at inventing ways to reimagine disorder as order. As I've said elsewhere, that's one of the things art and literature do well.[6]

Living inside shipwreck feels even less comfortable than being on "shipwreck alert." One key difference involves intensifying attitudes toward change. In alert, we're animated by paranoia and fantasies of structure, a frantic half-awareness and constant state of re-interpretation that I always associate with reading, or even more re-reading, one of Thomas Pynchon's early novels. We're pole-axed with dread, afraid of impending loss, melancholy with nostalgia for things we believe we have, or have only just lost, a short minute ago. But that's not what it's like inside disaster. Inside shipwreck, as the ship comes apart and water pours in, we've no time to waste and an urgent need to get used to being wet. To flesh out the structure in Pynchonian terms, the in-between state of shipwreck resembles the immersive Zone of *Gravity's Rainbow*, where we dimly glimpse or perhaps ourselves become part of the Counterforce. Shipwreck alert, by contrast, might be a more direct attempt to unmask a global conspiracy, like those that animate the early novels *V.* and *The Crying of Lot 49*. All of which puts Tommy P. on both sides of this divide, right where he'd want to be.

It may not be where we want to be, but it's where we are.

THE FIRST WRECK: NORTH HAVEN, CONNECTICUT, 1997

Shipwrecks are human stories, though they do not only involve humans. My own years of wrestling with this ancient narrative topos have many sources, including the memorable wrecking of a borrowed Hobie cat on jellyfish-filled Chesapeake Bay in August 1988. (Misjudging the swell, I sunk the cat's pontoon and pole-vaulted us into jellied waters. Swimming after the boat was like dancing through an angry

Anthropocene. Further speculations about the meanings of and alternatives to this term will appear in my next book, *Shipwreck and the Global Ecology*, forthcoming from University of Minnesota Press.
[6] See "Tongues in the Storm: Shakespeare, Ecological Crisis, and the Resources of Genre," *Ecocritical Shakespeare*, ed. Lynne Bruckner and Dan Brayton (Aldershot: Ashgate, 2011), 155–172.

Smucker's jar.) In academic life, my shipwreck love surfaced when I went to see that horrible movie with Leo and Kate. Early in the spring of 1997, in the company of my wife's then-teenage cousins, we went to see James Cameron's block-buster at a suburban multiplex in North Haven. The cousins, self-named *Titaniacs*, had already been perhaps ten or more times, but we had until then resisted.

For the first hour or more, I squirmed in my seat. The writing was excruciating, the performances hackneyed, the plot—such as it was—too brittle to bear. I still can hardly stand to remember it now: the card-playing painter, unhap-py young wife, evil plutocrat who might as well have been twisting his waxed mustachios. It was so painful that I've resisting seeing it ever again, despite sixteen years of re-calling and reconsidering that singular viewing.

At some point, close to halfway through, the ship hit the iceberg. That's when shipwreck got its bait between my teeth. I bit, disaster set the hook, and I was on the line. Since then I've been struggling. I'm getting used to it.

The drama of shipwreck, it turns out, has a narrative force and propulsion that can carry even the schlockiest of stories. Images of the great wounded ship, the icy water, straining machinery, and flooding ballrooms, nearly made up for, or at least obscured, the syrupy melodrama. Ignoring the story, I ate up the scenery. At that time I was writing a dissertation about narrative romance, in its classical, Byzan-tine, and Renaissance incarnations, so I'd been thinking about shipwreck as, in Northrop Frye's phrase, a "standard means of transportation" in these long-lived narrative forms.[7] What I hadn't realized was how much work the shipwreck could do by itself, inside a mangled narrative.

I think about that turning point often. Shipwreck grabbed me that evening, reached out and claimed me through dreck and cinematic detritus. It didn't make me King of the World, but it's given me lots to think about. I've imagined coming into the theater ninety minutes late, not knowing or caring about Kate or Leo. What kind of story is a story of only-disaster, powerful enough to obscure sentiment and a cheesy

[7] Northrop Frye, *The Secular Scripture: A Study of the Structure of Romance* (Cambridge: Harvard University Press, 1978). The fruit of my own work on Greek and Elizabethan prose romance is *Romance for Sale in Early Modern England* (Aldershot: Ashgate, 2006).

love story? Is it a story that anyone but me would want to watch? If you don't care about the humans, is it still a ship-wreck?

THE SECOND WRECK: UNITED STATES, SEPTEMBER 11, 2012

The release date was September 10 in London, but American listeners like me had to wait to download the new Dylan album until 9/11/12. The title track, "Tempest," hit me with the weight of my musical hero laying down my own obsession. There in the cold water with the great ship on April 15, 1912—I'm not conspiratorial about dates, but look at all those nines, ones, and twos—Dylan growled out his oceanic parable. There was nothing explicit about the 9/11 anniversary in the album's pre-release publicity, and no clear references to the twenty-first century catastrophe in the songs, but the timing seems pointed. The Titanic, like 9/11, marks a hinge-moment in Anglo-American culture's historical imagination. These disasters remade our collective historical narratives. The loss of the ocean liner marked the end of European triumphalism and the start of the general disaster at the center of which lay the Great War. The attacks of 9/11/01 initiated a new phase of American and global politics, the so-called "War on Terror." It's typical of Dylan's obliquity that he might respond to 9/11 by way of the Titanic. The song performs a time-knot of multiple historicities, gesturing at once toward 1912, 2001, and 2012. The careful balancing of the album's American release date of 9/11/12 reaches back in its day and month to the early twenty-first century terror attack while its calendar year recalls the century that had passed since the Titanic's voyage. As a chrono-hinge swinging both ways, Dylan's shipwreck song hits multiple temporalities.

My reading of Dylan's "Tempest" traces the almost-too-obvious Shakespearean parallels and suggests that the song traps its audience just where I want to be, inside the revelatory chaos of shipwreck. Dylan snarled at a reporter who asked him if the title "Tempest" indicated that this would be his final album: "Shakespeare's last play was called *The Tempest*. It wasn't called just plain 'Tempest.' The name of my record is just plain 'Tempest.' It's two different titles."[8]

---

[8] Mikhal Gilmore, "Bob Dylan on Dark New Album, Tempest," *Roll-*

The angry denial seems unbelievable, but it helps clarify that Dylan's song, which takes place almost entirely on the doomed ship, maps out an almost perfect inverse of Shakespeare's play, which contains only one scene on board a ship that does not, finally, sink. There is no tempestuous storm in Dylan, and no real wreck in Shakespeare. The song's gesture toward Shakespeare's not-quite-final play hints at how we should read Dylan's dark waltz.[9]

The quasi-supernatural figure of "the watchman," who appears four times in the song to guide maritime disaster into artistic order, is Dylan's Prospero, his wizard and presiding figure. "The watchman, he lay dreaming . . ." goes the refrain. His dream, like Prospero's magic, controls the action: "He dreamed the Titanic was sinking" (stanza 45).[10] The four watchman stanzas transform disaster into story, distant knowledge into bodily experience, epic possibility into unanswered need. Like Shakespeare's Prospero, the watchman hovers above the action, controlling, or pretending to control, the action. The movement across these four stanzas takes us from "ballroom dancers" and "the underworld" (stanza 6) to the watchman's and ship's bodies titled together "at forty-five degrees" (stanza 16). Next we recognize that "the damage had been done" despite our a futile desire "to tell someone" (stanza 37), and finally, in the concluding stanza (45), we discern a vision of loss and possibility.

He watches, but he can't tell.

In the historical metaphor, the watchman is the crewman who missed the iceberg. By emphasizing impotence and failure, this figure demotes Prospero from controlling mage to passive dreamer. Shakespeare's wizard dramatizes fantasies of power, but Dylan's watchman seals this figure up in an isolated crow's nest. He has nothing to do but watch. The four moments in which Dylan brings his watchman forward pull his song momentarily up from the raw experience of disaster, inviting the consolations or transformations of art.

---

ing Stone, Aug 16, 2012: http://www.rollingstone.com/music/news/bob-dylan-on-his-dark-new-album-tempest-20120801.

[9] As Dylan and many other people apparently don't know, Shakespeare wrote or co-wrote at least a few more plays after *The Tempest*, though all of our dates for his plays are unreliable.

[10] Dylan did not publish the song's lyrics, but a transcription is readily available on the web: http://rock.genius.com/Bob-dylan-tempest-lyrics#lyric. Citations in the text by stanza number.

But this wizard isn't in control.

When the song takes us down from the watchman's heights below the decks of the doomed ship, its chaos and overabundance unpack the felt experience of maritime chaos. Shipwrecks are always hard to narrate, but Dylan's song takes special pleasure in plunging into disorder. At its center is human incomprehension; that's the largest meaning of Dylan's shipwreck. He belts out his key hermeneutic phrase, "there is no understanding" (stanza 43), like a self-explanatory proverb. Fourteen minutes and forty-five stanzas can't clean up the disorder.

Human meaning-making systems cannot encompass this oceanic chaos. As another Shakespearean daughter bullies her father into acknowledging, the only human response is sympathy: "O, I have suffered / With those that I saw suffer!" (*The Tempest*, 1.2.5–6). Miranda asks her wizard-watchman-father to feel with her, and with us, to attune ourselves to what sailors fear. Dylan's "Tempest," on the other hand, sings Miranda down:

> They waited at the landing
> And they tried to understand
> But there is no understanding
> For the judgments of God's hand (stanza 43)

No understanding. God's hand behind the wizard's curse. This stanza bristles with Bob's Jeremiah thunder-growl, but it also sounds oddly freeing. What happens if we give up on understanding? Might it mean we don't have to be on alert anymore? That we can turn, instead, to something else?

No understanding fixes a bleak sentiment at the heart of this long song, and maybe it's just me who hears aesthetic hope in these lines. But I don't think Dylan's shipwreck leaves us in despair. That's not the final force of its shipwreck ecology. What if we turn from things that aren't working— from watchmen who can't act and from failed human understanding—and focus instead on overflowing abundance? Everybody's there on board the doomed ship with us. The movie star shows up early: "Leo took his sketchbook / He was often so inclined" (stanza 7).[11] Dylan happily copped to

---

[11] The Rock Genius website also notes that Leo Zimmerman was a historical passenger on the Titanic, and that Bob Dylan's given name

the pop-culture reference. "Yeah, Leo," he admitted to *Rolling Stone*, "I didn't think the song would be the same without him. Or the movie."[12] The star pairs up with rhyming Cleo, who might be Shakespeare's Egyptian heroine or Leo's leading lady. They mingle with Wellington and Jim Dandy, Calvin, Blake, and Wilson—the theologian, poet, and American president?—Davy the brothel-keeper, Jim Backus and the bishop, even "the rich man, Mr Aster." The story unfolds through excess—who ever heard of a fourteen-minute pop song, much less a waltz? It's too much, too many fragments of story and experience and feeling. But it all adds up to something. The song sings it out—

The ship was going under
The universe had opened wide. (stanza 12)

There's a basic eco-point amid the flotsam. Shipwreck names the core experience, the shock and pressure of the inhuman world on human skin. Being-in-the-world means living inside shipwreck. It's the story we need to explain, can't explain, and must tell. A direct encounter: ocean liner meets iceberg, human bodies splash into cold salt water. We want and can't have distance, perspective, narrative, a story that explains and insulates.

We want the source. Tell me the cause, Muse! But we never get it.

The wetness of the encounter, the brute physicality of shipwreck, won't let us understand causes. This song, this disaster, the oceanic histories and snatches of poetry that events like the Titanic open up, resonate without rest. The only apparent stability is on the sea floor, but that distant space is also a churning site of sea changes fast and slow.

A shipwreck ecology, however, needn't be a place only of horror or nostalgia. There's ecstasy in the waters, too. Not the relief of having survived or the satisfaction of figuring it out: those things don't last. But an intellectual tingle that ripples out into the physical world, a willingness to confront the inhumanity of our environment, and an appetite for experience that doesn't mind getting wet. That's the direction named reality. And ecology. Also shipwreck.

is Robert Zimmerman.
[12] Gilmore, "Bob Dylan on Dark New Album."

THE THIRD WRECK: CALIFORNIA AS LEMURIA IN *INHERENT VICE* (2009)

Moving from Bob Dylan to Thomas Pynchon shouldn't be hard. They share a shipwreck aesthetic, a taste for disorder, and a rage against history. They are each, in their different modes—Dylan as gnomic rock star, Pynchon as obsessively publicity-averse novelist—among the greatest living American writers associated with the cultural upheavals of the 1960s. Their lives even almost overlapped for a while in the early 1960s, when Pynchon's college buddy Richard Fariña was married to Mimi Baez and Dylan was living with Mimi's sister Joan.[13] Pynchon's farewell to youthful idealism has had its ups and downs, as has Dylan's, but his most recent novel, *Inherent Vice* (2009), paints an indulgent caricature of the 1960s in Southern California. The novel retells modern American history as a shipwreck survival story, with the tragic outcome never in doubt. It's impossible, as Pynchon's readers know, to stay dry and uncontaminated in his near-historical world. In this novel, the private eye hero, Doc Sportello, staggers through a sex-drugs-and-paranoia-filled odyssey spiraling out from his pad in Gordita Beach—a loosely allegorized version of Manhattan Beach, where Pynchon lived in the late 1960s and early 1970s—across the Southland from Los Angeles to Las Vegas. A great conspiratorial catastrophe looms off-stage, as it so often does in Pynchon's novels, in this case associated with a maritime cartel known as the Golden Fang, possibly engaged in running heroin from Southeast Asia, among other things. Historical jokes anticipate the birth of the Internet, via the novel's portrait of the web-precursor ARPA NET, and the rise of modern con-

---

[13] On these entangled lives, see David Hajdu's *Positively 4th Street: The Lives and Times of Joan Baez, Bob Dylan, Mimi Baez Fariña, and Richard Fariña* (New York: Farar, Straus and Guroux, 2001). Written with the apparent cooperation of Mimi Baez Fariña, the book is a bit of hatchet job on the young, ambitious, emotionally cruel Dylan. Pynchon, on the other hand, appears as a loyal friend to his college buddy Richard Fariña. For a summary of what is known about Pynchon's life, timed to promote his latest novel, *Bleeding Edge*, see Boris Kachka, "On the Thomas Pynchon Trail: From the Long Island of His Boyhood to the 'Yupper West Side' of His New Novel," *Vulture*, August 25, 2013: http://www.vulture.com/2013/08/thomas-pynchon-bleeding-edge.html.

servatism, via a few glancing jabs at Ronald Reagan.[14] The shipwreck at the novel's heart, however, is the long-ago sinking of the mythical continent of Lemuria beneath the Pacific. This half-hidden tragedy structures *Inherent Vice* like a submarine reef and connects the novel to Dylan's retelling of the Titanic disaster. For Pynchon as for Dylan, watery catastrophe builds a story of origins, reprising the fallen nature of the world. The loss of Lemuria drowns some primal historical innocence, some almost-forgotten possibility. Refugees from Lemuria, reports Doc's one-time receptionist Sortilège, whose name gestures toward the Roman method of divination by lots (*sortes*) that lead Augustine to Christianity and Jonah to be thrown into the sea, settled California, making that beachy utopian state, in Doc's awkward phrase, "like, a ark" (352). The fate of that ark, that mechanism for enduring shipwreck, shadows the novel's tales of ancient and modern disasters.

Inside a faux-detective novel that's as crowded and personality-suffused as Dylan's "Tempest," Pynchon inserts the legend of Lemuria as the "Atlantis of the Pacific" (101). The alternative oceanic history of this land inverts and opposes the power-politics of Atlantis, the Atlantic, and Western thought from Plato forward. Lemuria represents a Pacific and anti-European alternative symbology which features "spirit guide[s]" such as "Kamukea, a Lemuro-Hawaiian demigod from the dawn of the Pacific history, who centuries ago had been a sacred functionary of the lost continent now lying beneath the Pacific Ocean" (105). Hazy though its outlines may be, Lemuria's key symbolic force comes from its opposition to right-wing Atlantis. In this allegorical reading of history, "Nixon [was] a descendent of Atlantis just as Ho Chi Minh was of Lemuria, because for tens of thousands of years all wars in Indochina had really been proxy wars, going back . . . to the moment when three Lemurian holy men landed on these [California's] shores, fleeing the terrible inundation which had taken their homeland" (109). This alternative history of an ocean and continent without Europe, without empire, with only a stoner's paranoid historical connection to California, floats amid the disorder of Pynchon's novel, tantalizing his characters and readers with un-

[14] Thomas Pynchon, *Inherent Vice* (New York: Penguin, 2009) 53, 322. Further citations noted parenthetically in the text.

taken alternatives. Lemuria may never fully return, even though some hippies claim it's "rising to the surface again" (101), but it indicates something worth clinging to. The hidden shroud of the lost continent represents the novel's fantasy answer to the shipwreck of history.

Mostly hidden among the novel's terrestrial plots—a heady brew of crime, lost love, criminal real estate developments, drug smuggling, and the Golden Fang—Lemuria and its continental shipwreck occupy the utopian heart of *Inherent Vice*. As Sortilège tells Doc after revealing that she's been hearing voices from the vanished continent in her dreams, "it isn't just a place" (167). The names of the novel's two most important characters besides Doc, his ex-old lady Shasta Fay and his cop nemesis Bigfoot, both have Lemurian connections. New Agers claim that Mount Shasta marks the spot in California where the Lemurians first made landfall.[15] The mythical creature Bigfoot has also been reported to haunt remote Northern CA near Mt. Shasta.[16] Less overtly than the Golden Fang criminal conspiracy, which is apparently located on a boat that Doc never quite manages to reach, the Lemurian subtext links disparate elements of Pynchon's novel.

The key features of Lemuria, beyond its shipwreck-infused opposition to the forces of Anglo-European rectitude against which all of Pynchon's novels struggle, are its catastrophic hints at possible redemption. Pynchon's shipwreck story, more than Cameron's or Dylan's, imagines loss but also enmeshed survival. Lemuria, more than any other place, lives inside and through shipwreck. The penultimate and most utopian appearance of the lost Pacific continent comes

[15]See "About Mount Shasta," *The Lemurian Connection*," 2003-2009: http://www.lemurianconnection.com/category/about-mt-shasta. I found this bizarre New Age website via the very useful Pynchon wiki for *Inherent Vice*: http://inherent-vice.pynchonwiki.com/wiki/index. php?-title=Main_Page. Another pulp version of the Atlantis-Lemuria myth that Pynchon probably knows, because he knows everything, is the story of the warrior-king Kull, created by Robert E. Howard, who also invented the figure of Conan the Barbarian. See Robert E. Howard, *Kull* (1929; reprt. New York: Bantam, 1978).

[16] Or so the legend, and the *Mount Shasta Herald*, has it. See "Creature Spotted on Mt. Shasta" (*Mount Shasta Herald*, California, September 9, 1976), *Bigfoot Encounters*: http://www.bigfootencounters. com/articles/mtshasta.htm.

after Doc has been dreaming that "the schooner *Golden Fang* . . . had reassumed its old working identity, and well as its real name, *Preserved*" (340). This vision of redemption, of turning back the clock of catastrophic history, spills over into Doc's conversation with his buddy and sometime-lawyer Sauncho—cue the Cervantine soundtrack—who provides "a kind of courtroom summary" that brings together the Golden Fang and Lemuria:

> . . . yet there is no avoiding time, the sea of time, the sea of memory and forgetfulness, the years of promise, gone and unrecoverable, of the land almost allowed to claim its better destiny, only to have the claim jumped by evil-doers known all too well, and taken instead and held hostage to the future we must live in now forever. May we trust that this blessed ship is bound for some better shore, some undrowned Lemuria, risen and redeemed, where the American fate, mercifully, failed to transpire . . . . (341)

Sauncho's reverie fantasizes the transformation that Doc's dream previewed, that the criminal ship can re-become the preserver, Lemuria rise again, and America's fall into tragic history will have been avoided. The vision imagines a new kind of voyage—"From the beach Doc and Sauncho saw her, or thought they saw her, heading out to sea, all sails glowing and spread" (341)—but they're not sure if it's real. There's no certain route out of history in Pynchon, any more than a way off the ship in Dylan's "Tempest."

The oceanic fantasy Doc and Sauncho share doesn't close up the plot-tapestry of *Inherent Vice*, which in typical Pynchon fashion leaves plenty of loose threads hanging. In place of the anti-closure of *The Crying of Lot 49* or the only-rhetorical unity of *Gravity's Rainbow*, however, this self-consciously non-epic novel ends with a foggy vignette. Doc's driving south on the Santa Monica Freeway, heading back home to Gordita, when he encounters in coastal fog an allegorical mixture of water in air: "The third dimension grew less and less reliable . . . . At first the fog blew in separate sheets, but soon everything grew thick and uniform till all Doc could see were his headlight beams, like eyestalks of an extraterrestrial, aimed into the hushed whiteness ahead" (367). Like the (imagined?) ship *Golden Fang* bearing ex-zombie and surf-rock sax player Coy Harlington and his family to safety, the "hushed whiteness" of the fog stimulates a textual move from physical description to utopian imagination. Coy sails away under glowing sails, but in the coastal fog Doc and his fellow drivers inch along behind one another, their unspeaking cars "set[ting] up a temporary commune to help each other home through the fog" (368). It can't last, but Doc is well supplied, with "a container of coffee from Zucky's and almost a full pack of smokes" (368). Inside the fog—surrounded by a swirling, unseeable mixture of water and air, as if the ocean had come, briefly, ashore—he feels as if there's somewhere to go:

> Maybe . . . it would stay this way for days, maybe he'd have to just keep driving, down past Long Beach, down through Orange County, and San Diego, and across a border where nobody could tell anymore in the fog who was Mexican, who was Anglo, who was anybody. (369)

Fog creates an identityless, racially indistinct utopian community, a place outside of organized thought, recalling perhaps the "Mindless Pleasures" of Pynchon's original working title for *Gravity's Rainbow*. When you can't see, it can't matter all that much where you're headed. As Bob Dylan might put it, "there is no understanding." Which doesn't mean you can't keep heading south.

Old Pynchon hands know what happens next, know that it's the "temporary" that this writer loves even more than the "commune." Doc knows it won't last: "Then again, he might run out of gas before that happened, and have to leave the caravan, and pull over on the shoulder, and wait" (369). In this last tableau, stranded on the side of the road inside the fog, his car-ship transformed into a landed shipwreck, Doc stuck and static inside, Pynchon imagines, wistfully, that rescue might arrive. Doc's fantasies are predictable: a "forgotten joint," "the CHP," "a restless blonde in a Stingray" (369). Drugs, cops, sex. But what Doc really wants and dreads, Pynchon tells us, is for "the fog to burn away, and for something else this time, somehow, to be there instead" (369). After this foggy land-wreck, the hero waits for the reality that's always missing, always just beyond that next corner, waiting and unseen. Living in fog: when you can't see, how can you understand?

WHAT HAPPENS AT THE END?

Let's let Bob sing us away to the end, because there is no

home, no lasting arrival or looked-for port in a world of shipwreck:

The watchman he lay dreaming

What's a story if not a dream? I think back to that ordinary evening in North Haven, at the movies with the cousins-in-law, in that strange-to-remember world of my own historical past. I knew I wouldn't like *Titanic*. I was just going along with the family. So how did the big boat snag me, reach out through celluloid clichés to touch that part of me that stings and doesn't forget? Am I the watchman dreaming, or a lost soul on the boat?

Of all the things that can be

Bobbie D. knows what I love about shipwreck: there's nothing bigger. No trope vaster, more capacious, more emblematic while also being more painfully real. "All the things that can be" is a lot of things—but that's what us shipwreck-watchers dream. Everything's here, on board or by the boards, the water's rising, eyes open wide. The ocean comes up to meet us. The sea is history, says a poet.[17] It's slavery, counters a novelist.[18] It's Romanticism, intones another poet.[19] It's our hostile, salty, changing, inescapable world.

He dreamed the Titanic was sinking

Because what else would he dream, the man who watches? This is the basic matrix, the thing everything else comes from: a dreaming human and a sinking ship. What can the dreaming mind do with what we see? No understanding, the singer sings. No clear views in the fog, the novelist tells us. But the dreaming-sinking remains, we're representing the disaster while we're living through it. No way out but down.

Into the deep blue sea . . .

---

[17] Derek Walcott, "The Sea is History," *Selected Poems*, ed. Edward Baugh (New York: Farar, Straus and Giroux, 2007), 137.
[18] Fred D'Aguiar, *Feeding the Ghosts* (New York: Ecco, 2000), 1.
[19] W. H. Auden, *The Enchafed Flood, or the Romantic Iconography of the Sea* (London: Faber & Faber, 1951).

Just because we know our destination is no reason to think we're already there. The sea waits, blue and deep, salty as the tears in our eyes. Why hurry? Unless it's because we like the taste, the bitter smell of the wind at low tide, the crackling sensation of dried salt water on the skin of my back and arms, right now, this instant, while I'm typing I can feel it. The ocean's salt is on me. In the middle of all these words, all this representation, the physical thing is here. It's not only writing. It's here on my skin, as I sit and write and listen to Bob Dylan sing.

What would the ocean say back to the ship Titanic or to the movie, to the song "Tempest" or the play *The Tempest*? What would the sea say to our friend Thomas Pynchon, flowing up to his West Side haunts, embittering the Hudson with the incoming tide?

Shipwreck ecology means living with sea on skin.

HEWN

Anne F. Harris[1]

Hewn is a status in the ecology of the inhuman, a state of being that is as old as human presence outside of Eden. Its ancient word of origin, "hew," carries an onomatopoeic trace of the effort of cutting down, the blunt force seized by the body to bring down the thing. Hewing is a gesture of intervention and survival, one of several taught to Adam by Christ for his brave new world. Adam seems surprised in this 13th-century Bible Picture Book: his hands startling back into inaction, his foot slipping beyond the frame (Fig. 1). Christ pushes through, breaks the surface with certitude, and models the motion of ecological conquest. Thus, as the rubric above the image tells us, "Adam learns to labor the earth."[2]

[1] This essay is contributed with many thanks for the conversations that Jeffrey Cohen gathered around the ecology of the inhuman, in admiration of my fellow panelists and authors, and in gratitude to the friends and colleagues who encouraged this fascination with the hewn.
[2] "Adam aprend labourer terre." See Michael Camille, "'When Adam Delved': Laboring on the Land in English Medieval Art," in *Agriculture in the Middle Ages*, ed. Del Sweeney (Philadelphia: University of Pennsylvania Press, 1995), 247–276.

The hewn is the hospitable, Adam learns, and his reluctance will not keep him long from his own delving and hewing.

Figure 1. Christ Teaching Adam How to Delve. Cycle of Old and New Testament Images, Possibly Prefatory Cycle for a Psalter, c. 1250, fol. 3. 1915.533/E12682. Printed with permission of the Art Institute of Chicago.

To hew calls on both skill and calamity, mundane repetition in the field and final blow in battle. Ask Adam; then ask Cain. Troublingly, the word oscillates between different kinds of violence throughout its medieval use. There is the matter of men: of Abel, and helmets and hauberks hewed as late as Malory;[3] and there is the matter of trees and stones: of forests cleared, and stones quarried and cut, and Paradise

[3] Oxford English Dictionary (OED), Vol. 7, 2nd edn. (Oxford: Clarendon Press, 1989), 194.

Lost. The human and the inhuman both tumble. Both can be hewn, and language pushes us to examine the fallen in these realms we try so hard to keep apart.[4] The hewn body becomes the principal object in the hero's funerary rites. Hewn wood becomes the animate crucifix that speaks in the miracle. This essay will focus on the hewn element that becomes bodily, more than the body that becomes the hewn element. But there is much simultaneity in this word and its offshoots that challenges the separation it enacts.

Hewing is a *de-cision*, as Michel Serres understands the word in discussing Genesis, "express[ing] cutting, the creation of an edge."[5] To hew is to seek to assert the edge, the break, that mastery. The "hewster," obsolete in language if not in practice, cleared land—cut down to create, and labored for an ecology of hewn things, a world of discrete entities and firm decisions. Or so goes the fantasy of the hewster. The *act* of hewing tries to create boundaries between part and whole, living and dead, and animate, and inanimate. But the *existence* of the hewn travels back and forth over these boundaries. We have relegated the hewn to the inhuman: we call it inanimate, cut off, isolated. But the hewn can yearn for the whole, can insistently tend towards it, and remembers it in parts. It is the element that is still connected, indiscrete, despite our best efforts at separation and distinction. This ecology of hewn things that we live within is filled with potential remembrances. They mark the trajectory away from Eden and plenitude, and into our fragmented existence.

The hewn becomes the inhuman. It is the thing after the cutting: wood after tree; statue after stone; jewel after gem. It lurches its way from one state of being to another: first the violent hewing gesture, then the care and refinement, the shaping into human ritual and pleasure. All this is preceded by the time-before-human-perception of the hewn when it was whole. Its temporality chronicles a not-quite-absolute transformation. The ambiguity of the hewn's linguistic permutations will not let us settle into just one meaning: as

---

[4] See Tim Ingold, "Anthropology Comes to Life," in *Being Alive; Essays on Movement, Knowledge and Description* (New York: Routledge), 3–14, especially the idea that "the very concept of the 'human' seems to embody the abiding paradox of a form of life that can realize its own essence only by transcending it" (8).

[5] Michel Serres, *The Natural Contract*, trans. Elizabeth MacArthur and William Paulson (Ann Arbor: University of Michigan Press, 2011), 52.

much as we hew statue from stone, the statue *hews unto* its stoniness. We value it for doing so; we want the original element to assert itself through the form we've imposed upon it. The wonder of the hewn is in its blended ontology: its ability to be both wood *and* tree, while being separate things. The temporality of the hewn is intimately intertwined in its ontology: the before and after of multiple gestures (cutting, shaping, reorienting) bespeak multiple states of being.[6] There is a spectrum here: from work of art to detritus—things hewn and strewn.

What happens in the ontological trajectory from stone to statue, from tree to wood? From tree to wood to cross? And, displacing the human agency in all this: what is the perception of that trajectory by the hewn thing? At what point does the statue stare back at its maker? To whom does the Holy Rood speak? We could say that having been cut down, the hewn becomes the plaything of our imagination, and that it becomes an object of contemplation or revulsion. Or, we could consider that in being cut down, the hewn gains the agency of a thing,[7] a complicated thing that recalls its whole by being a part, a kind of thing that becomes an actant with memory.

The hewn acts upon the human, simultaneously bearing witness to what had been whole, and calling out for more manipulations and further fragmentations. In this generative capacity is a realization that things are not static, that they are better called, in Ian Bogost's phrase, "unit operations."[8] They act as one among and with multiples. They interact with other unit operations, they become other things, and they tend towards one another: the stone with other statues

[6] Vin Nardizzi, *Wooden Os: Shakespeare's Theatres and England's Trees* (Toronto: University of Toronto Press, 2013). In his fascinating study of "a series of ligneous transformations" (137), Nardizzi explores the multiple ontologies and temporalities of stage trees extending from the increasingly scarce woodlands of early modern England to the forest fantasies of London theaters (and even perhaps to the tenements of urban dwellers after the theaters were taken down).

[7] See Bill Brown, "Thing Theory," *Critical Inquiry* 28.1 (Autumn 2001): 1–22, especially the dynamic of "[o]n the one hand, then, the thing baldly encountered. On the other, some thing not quite apprehended" (5).

[8] Ian Bogost, "Unit Operations," in *Alien Phenomenology, or What It's Like to Be a Thing* (Minneapolis: University of Minnesota Press, 2012), 22–29.

and structures and settings, the cross with further crucifixions and embellishments and sacraments. Hewing sets things into different kinds of motions: more immobilizing ones will hew to and attachment to tradition, others will quicken with the possibilities of cutting and new forms. The rock quarry and the forest are bristling with life, and we would be wrong to think we render it inanimate when we cut and hew our way through.[9] The hewn is lively: it is not static, nor is it isolated: detritus captivates the imagination of Jane Bennett in its interactions, assemblages, and associations.[10] Similarly, on the other end of the spectrum of value imposed by humans, works of art, no matter how high the pedestal, contain and embody their raw materials, their makers' gestures, and their owners' desire.

With the objects of the *Arma Christi* and the voice of the *Dream of the Rood* I seek to engage in the kind of carpentry that Ian Bogost invites: "constructing artifacts that illustrate the perspectives of objects."[11] Both constructions position objects to operate beyond human reach, and to create otherworldly spaces: the eerily quiet space of the *Arma Christi* gathering around the Wound of Christ; and the dreamscape of the Rood's remembering. They establish ecologies in which the intentions of the inhuman shape the environment. What the wound *tends to*, what the wood *tends towards*: these are the pursuits of a hewn ecology. Less anthropomorphic than asking what things want, this line of inquiry traces what things intend: what they incline towards, what they might attract or gather unto themselves, and how they pull towards

---

[9] Eduardo Kohn, *How Forests Think: Towards an Anthropology Beyond the Human* (Berkeley: University of California Press, 2013). In his co-existence within and study of the world of the Avila Runa in the Ecuadorian Amazon, Kohn describes a "multinatural" forest of physical and spiritual signification (156). Engaging semiotics with eco-criticism, Kohn's book argues for patterns, which he also calls "forms," in the forest that are read, interpreted, and acted upon by human and beyond-human actants simultaneously in an ever-transforming series of "trans-species intimacies" (153–154). See specifically "Forms' Effortless Efficacy," 153–188.

[10] Jane Bennett, "The Agency of Assemblages," in *Vibrant Matter: A Political Ecology of Things* (Durham: Duke University Press, 2010), 20–38, especially the theory of "distributive agency" that Bennett develops in her consideration of an "agentic assemblage" (21), such as an electrical power grid, or, here, a devotional *Arma Christi* page/image.

[11] Bogost, *Alien Phenomenology*, 109.

other unit operations. Separate, fragmented, and suspended, the *Arma Christi* and the Rood project the perspective of objects outside of the human agency of narrative and action, even as it invites and involves them. The agency of the hewn lies in the intention of its objects.

ARMA CHRISTI: SUSPENSION/SCALE

The *Arma Christi* are commonly found in late medieval Books of Hours—ontographic interruptions in an otherwise wordy environment, exploded diagrams of the Passion holding its objects in ontological suspension. All is hewn here: cut off from narrative, separate in space, indeterminate in time, and singular in intention—sponge, bucket, tomb, whip, nail—the very page of the manuscript is cut from lambskin. They initiate an instrumentalization of devotion, in which *things* dominate, and exist in an insistent present, within a visual field otherwise filled with the human emotion and chaos of the Crucifixion.[12] In the depiction of the *Arma Christi*, however, it is the unit operations of hammer, ladder, rope, and spear that guide the eye and mind (Fig. 2). The ecology of the hewn here creates an environment of spiritual exploration of the viewer, aligning common objects made sacred by stillness and juxtaposition, provoking a dynamic of personal thoughts beyond the common narrative.[13] In their valorization of objects, the *Arma Christi* initially reduce or

[12] The recent publication of the anthology, *The Arma Christi in Medieval and Early Modern Material Culture; with a Critical Edition of 'O Vernicle,'* eds. Lisa H. Cooper and Andrea Denny-Brown (Burlington: Ashgate, 2014), offers an expansive range of discussions and images of the *Arma Christi* from Cynewulf to Hieronymus Bosch, from the "proto-*Arma Christi*" of Paul's Early Christianity to the doctrinal debates of Michelangelo's late Renaissance. Citing the "thing-power" and "active, earth, not-quite-human capaciousness" of objects delineated by Jane Bennett in *Vibrant Matter*, the editors note "the mystery of the sensed-yet-not-quite-graspable material force of the *arma*" (4; from their Introduction "*Arma Christi:* The Material Culture of the Passion," 1–19).

[13] Ann Eljenholm Nichols, "'O Vernicle': Illustrations of an *Arma Christi* Poem," in *Tributes to Kathleen L. Scott: English Medieval Manuscripts and Their Readers*, eds. Marlene Villalobos Henessey (New York: Brepols, 2009), discussing the more linear presentations of the *Arma Christi* found in scrolls, argues for the objects as "focal points not for meditation on the Passion but rather for an examination of conscience" (143).

occlude the human: Christ's body is markedly absent, excised from the gathering of objects. [14] But, the reduction of Christ to a Wound arguably intensifies his suffering and presence, localizes and situates his pain as an undeniable thing. In the devotional logic of the hewn, metonymy amplifies.

Figure 2. The Holy Wound of Christ flanked by the "arma Cristi." From the Psalter and Hours of Bonne of Luxembourg, Duchess of Normandy, Fol. 331r. France, Paris; before 1349. Tempera, grisaille, ink, and gold leaf on vellum. Individual folios: 4 15/16 x 3 9/16 in. (12.6 x 9 cm) The Cloisters Collection, 1969 (69.86). Printed with permission from Art Resource.

[14] When Christ's body appears on an *Arma Christi* page, as it will when Arma Christi iconography is combined with that of the Mass of Saint Gregory, it becomes one object among many: prized and centralized, but also stilled and suspended.

Narrative hovers around the edges, looking for a way in (perhaps through the viewer's imagination or knowledge), but never coalescing to organize the objects into a story. Does the ecology of the hewn resist narrative? Without necessarily contesting human involvement, because the things do present themselves with visual clarity, it slips the hold of the human organizational tactic of narrative. The hewn can be identified, but it is more difficult to narrativize, because it exists in a profoundly inhuman space and time: non-linear, perpetually suspended, unaligned, and outside of language. It is *recuperated* into language by eager human interlocutors, but it *exists* in thingness. The visual field of the manuscript page that holds these unit operations in suspension is itself a unit operation, a complex one involving animal death in its production and human desire in its reception. In discussing images of the wound of Christ, Martha Easton cautions against confusing "pictures drawn in the mind, and artistic representations."[15] I want to use this distinction to clear some space for the image of the *Arma Christi* to be a *physical* image, a series of disparate things in different ontological states (from animal skin, to ground up plant pigments, to egg yolk to gold leaf to crown of thorns to lance to column), in complex relationships of metaphors and sympathy with human spiritual needs—all the while realizing the inextricability of the hewn and the human. The hewn wouldn't exist without the human to hack it down, and yet images like the *Arma Christi* argue for a life of things after the cutting down. Suspension does not preclude, but nor does it prioritize, a relational existence with the human. Objects hover, in perpetual waiting and potential activation, in relation with each other only through scale.

Scale holds most of the objects in the image together, gathering them around the Wound. It allows for the objects to relate to each other outside of narrative. Whip is aligned to column, sponge to cross, Wound to column. But even scale shifts, as objects jostle for position: Wound outsizes word, human monumentalizes bird, nails diminish ladder. Objects relate not in use, or in the usefulness of narrative, but in what

[15] Martha Easton, "The Wound of Christ, the Mouth of Hell: Appropriations and Inversions of Female Anatomy in the Later Middle Ages," in *Tributes to Jonathan J.G. Alexander: The Making and Meaning of Illuminated Medieval and Renaissance manuscripts, Art and Architecture*, eds. Susan L'Engle and Gerald B. Guest (New York: Harvey Miller, 2006), 397.

scale calls attention to: shape, fit, and color. Scale collapses in the middle of the page, as the wound of Christ (hewn from the body of the hewed) draws itself up the center of the page, disrupting the fragile illusion of nearly analogous scale and almost coherent space, prompting questions about narrative and time, and reasserting the objecthood of every thing. The Wound is a spectacle of scale: outsized and outrageous, disruptive of the unity of objects within human scale, revelatory of the power of things.

The amplification of the Wound announces its power first to disrupt the visual field: to outsize every thing else and claim a pride of place in color and scale. This agency both represents and perpetuates the power of the wound of Christ in human devotion, so much so that, in the proliferation of its fecund objecthood, it becomes a thing that escapes human control. The complex ontological process through which Wound becomes Thing, an independent object with its own location and movements independent of the body of Christ whence it was hewn, is materialized in images. The Wound is pried from the body of Christ by the human desire to enter it; it becomes a thing by being insistently aligned with other things, it exemplifies the power of things to create—not the like-begets-like dynamic of nature/biology, but instead the associative tendency of things gathered in scale, suspension, and juxtaposition. Caroline Walker Bynum traces the multiplicity of things the Wound becomes on its way to being an independent unit operation: door, window, chalice, building, gateway, tower, dovecot, chalice, cavern.[16] Karma Lochrie and Amy Hollywood uncover further things the Wound becomes: breast, vagina, blood, milk, a "glorious slit."[17] It isn't just the human imagination that conjures up the next thing: the Wound's openness calls forth the doors, its protection the dovecote, its fluidity the blood. In the unit

---

[16] Caroline Walker Bynum, "Violence Occluded: The Wound in Christ's Side in Late Medieval Devotion," in *Feud, Violence and Practice: Essays in Medieval Studies in Honor of Stephen D. White*, eds. Belle S. Tuten and Tracey L. Ballado (Burlington: Ashgate, 2010), 95–116.

[17] Karma Lochrie, "Mystical Acts, Queer Tendencies," in *Constructing Medieval Sexuality*, eds. Karma Lochrie, Peggy McCracken, and James A. Schultz (Minneapolis: University of Minnesota Press, 1997), 180–200; Amy Hollywood, "'That glorious slit': Irigaray and the Medieval Devotion to Christ's Side Wound," in *Luce Irigaray and Premodern Culture: Thresholds of History*, eds. Theresa Krier and Elizabeth D. Harvey (New York: Routledge, 2004), 105–125.

operation of the Wound as passage, salvation and nurture create a complex ecology inter-related by thing qualities of scale and juxtaposition. Thus can a dovecot and a chalice co-exist.[18] The *material* image of the Wound is also generative. The Wound proliferates beyond the boundary of the manuscript to the multiplicity of prints and woodcuts. David S. Areford has linked the "exact repeatability of [the] medium" to an authentication of the Wound, and thus to its power in late medieval devotion.[19] In its strange tension between lost origin and future projection, the hewn exercises its power in its ability to be a multiplicity of things: wound, gateway, milk, lambskin, paper, even birthing charm.[20]

In that litanies are at their origin prayers of supplication, the Latour litany that can be enunciated by speaking the objects of the *Arma Christi* performs the salvific function of the manuscript within which it is embedded.[21] An *Arma Christi* page invites enunciation and supplication of both the hu-

[18] Silke Tammen, "Blick und Wunde—Blick und Form: zur Deuteungsproblematik der Seiten Wunde Christi in der Spätmittelalterlichen Buchmalerei," in *Bild und Körper im Mittelalter*, eds. Kristin Marek et al. (Munich: Wilhelm Fink Verlag, 2006), 85–114, traces the formal similarities of the Wound in its multiple presentations.

[19] David S. Areford, "Printing the Side Wound of Christ," in *The Viewer and the Printed Image in Late Medieval Europe* (Burlington: Ashgate, 2010), 229–267.

[20] First explored by W. Sparrow Simpson, "On the Measure of the Wound in the Side of the Redeemer, Worn Anciently as a Charm and on the Five Wounds as Represented in Art," *Journal of the British Archaeological Association* 30 (1874): 357–374. The Wound of Christ as birthing has more recently been studied by Flora Lewis, "The Wound in Christ's Side and the Instruments of the Passion: Gendered Experience and Response," in *Women and the Book: Assessing the Visual Experience*, eds. Lesley Smith and Jane H.M. Taylor (Toronto: University of Toronto Press, 1996), 216–217, and by Caroline Walker Bynum, *Christian Materiality: An Essay on Religion in Late Medieval Europe* (Cambridge: M.I.T. Press, 2011), 195–208.

[21] "Latour litany" is a term coined by Ian Bogost and articulated in *Alien Phenomenology* to indicate the disorienting phenomenon of the juxtaposition of disparate objects when they are merely *listed* alongside each other. In the reader's disorientation and inability to impose order (e.g. narrative, morality, aesthetics), the objects assert and associate themselves in a variety of interesting ways. Bogost invites readers to this experience at his Latour Litanizer: http://www.bogost.com/blog/latour_litanizer.shtml. The power of the *Arma Christi* to "litanize," to supplicate through lists, emerges from the viewer's necessary disorientation before the divine.

man and inhuman, as the two continue to circle around the hewn. The human speaks prayers through the hewn things of the *Arma Christi* and the Wound, and in these prayers is transformed through a process Michael Camille has called "mimetic identification."[22] As the Wound is a chalice, the supplicant draws closer to Christ through his Wound, the blood, the chalice, the spear—all the hewn things. But we need to ask now about how the things themselves draw closer to each other: what they tend to, what their tendencies are. In the absence of human presence, we can ask, "What does wood want?" There is a risk of anthropomorphic ventriloquism here, but I think that we can use the mediated representations of prayer and poem as part of the "carpentry of things" that unseal the desires of the inhuman.

THE DREAM OF THE ROOD: TENDENCY/INTENTION

We can still see the wood of the Cross speak in stone as a tree. The runes on the east and west sides of the Ruthwell Cross inscribe prized lines to be found in the poem the *Dream of the Rood*, wherein the Cross remembers itself as wood and calls itself forth as bejeweled reliquary (Fig. 3).[23] The ecology of the hewn is one of shifting materialities and serialized ontologies: tree becomes wood becomes Cross on stone carved with vines and animals. Each materialization manifests a new identity, a new function, a new being. These are disparate but not disconnected: they involve the Cross's human interlocutors, from the men who hewed it down, to Christ

[22] Michael Camille, "Mimetic Identification and Passion Devotion in the Later Middle Ages: A Double-Sided Panel by Meister Franke," in *The Broken Body: Passion Devotion in Late-Medieval Culture*, eds. A.A. MacDonald, H.N.B. Ridderbos, and R.M. Schlusemann (Groningen: Egbert Forsten, 1998), 183–210.

[23] Verses 39–49 on the east side describe the raising of the Cross, while verses 56b–65a on the west side describe its deposition. The Ruthwell Cross was raised around 700, but recent scholarship argues that the runic verses of the *Dream of the Rood* were added, possibly around the year 1000 (when the *Dream of the Rood* appears in full as an Anglo-Saxon poem in the *Vercelli Book*). See Paul Mayvaert "A New Perspective on the Ruthwell Cross: Ecclesia and Vita Monastica," in *The Ruthwell Cross; Papers from the Colloquium sponsored by the Index of Christian Art*, ed. Brendan Cassidy (Princeton University Press, 1992), 95–166; and Patrick W. Conner, "The Ruthwell Monument Runic Poem in a Tenth-Century Context," *The Review of English Studies* 59:238 (November 2007): 25–51.

who will be nailed upon it, to the worshipper who stands
before the Ruthwell Cross to read or hear its runes. Hewing
oscillates between separation and adherence here: the tree is
cut down and cut off from the forest, but the Cross takes on
Christ, and the adherents of the faith hew to the Crucifix.

Figure 3. Ruthwell Cross, west face, by 'Dougsim.' Licensed under
Creative Commons Attribution-Share Alike 3.0 via Wikimedia
Commons.

In writing "Orientations Matter," Sarah Ahmed examines
how an object (hers is a fellow object initially made of wood,
a table) may shape an orientation to the world; how it may
guide how a world unfolds in perception. My exploration of
the multiple unfoldings of the Cross as it moves from tree to

wood to cross to reliquary to sign is very much formed by her idea that "while bodies do things, things might also 'do bodies.'"[24] The Cross's agency is deeply linked to its shifting ontology: its ability to bear Christ upon itself, to appear to the dreamer of the *Dream of the Rood* poem, and to ventriloquize itself through the reading of the viewer of the Ruthwell Cross relies upon its presence as wood, image, and stone. Just as the bodies of Christ, the dreamer, and the viewer all "do things" with and to the Cross, so does the Cross "do" their bodies: the body of Christ is borne by the Cross and its suffering is underscored, supported, and amplified by the Cross's suffering; the dreamer's body is moved to understanding the suffering of Christ upon the Cross through the Cross's description of its own suffering; and the viewer's body is moved around the monument of the Cross by the rune's movements along the stones' edges.[25] Each ontological shift of the Cross provokes a re-orientation in perception, each new materialization "does" the bodies that manipulate it anew.

The runes that gird the Ruthwell Cross, describe the ascent of the Cross on one side, and its deposition on the other. They move along the stone's edges, delineating surge and contour. They gather the Cross unto itself, proclaim its emotions, and project its action. In language visually and culturally distinct from the Latin that frames the other surfaces of the Ruthwell Cross, the runes give voice to the Cross's fascination as the "young hero" (39) climbs it.[26] The Cross speaks

[24] Sarah Ahmed, "Orientations Matter," in *New Materialisms: Ontology, Agency, and Politics*, eds. Diana Coole and Samantha Frost (Durham: Duke University Press, 2010), 245.

[25] The assimilation of human body and cross is manifested as early as Tertullian in his description of the gesture of the sign of the cross over the body. For the highlighting an instance in which the human and the hewn (the body and the material culture with which it surrounds itself) overtake each other, see John Rumple, "'Take Up the Cross' (Mark 8:34 and par.): The History and Function of the Cross Saying in Earliest Christianity" (D.Phil., University of Edinburgh, 2008), where he claims that "[i]f making a cross sign did develop contemporaneously with other material and visual Christian symbols it would be impossible to determine from current data which of the forms came first, or which influenced the other's development" (275).

[26] Quotations, cited parenthetically by line number, of *Dream of the Rood* are from *Old and Middle English, c. 890-c. 1450: An Anthology*, ed. Elaine Treharne (London: Blackwell, 2010), 122–124.

its desire: "I trembled when the warrior embraced me" (42). This shudder is a moment of transformation: epiphany, erotics, mimetic identification. For when Christ's flesh is pierced with nails, so is the wood of the Cross; when Christ's blood flows from his body, the Cross feels itself being drenched, the blood seeping into its own vibrant flesh. "They mocked us both together" (48), it recalls at the end of the eastern Ruthwell rune, its remembrance of desire now an identification of sameness. Simultaneously, the Cross's steadfastness, which it claims from its treeness, characterizes Christ's strength. "I had to stand fast" (43), resolves the Cross, and "I did not dare to bend down" (45). Christ, too, "ascended on the high gallows" (40) and does not falter from his place, regardless of the nails and the blood and the pain. In a mimetic exchange of sensations, Christ and the Cross become entangled: anthropomorphism becomes arboreomorphism.

The Cross stays with Christ as long as it can. It suffers with Christ while he lives, and then, once Christ is dead, it becomes a witness: "I beheld all that" (58), reads the rune of the west face of the Ruthwell Cross. The hewn *bears* witness to suffering. Every hewn thing carries and proclaims the act of cutting down. Witnessing becomes heroic commemoration on the west side of the Ruthwell Cross, when both the Cross and Christ, as Maidie Hilmo has argued, take on "the last stand of the noble warrior."[27] Mimetic identification folds both Christ and the Cross into a heroic stance: now the image of the warrior comes forth and the deposition of the Cross/Christ, one "all wounded with arrows" (62) the other "weary-limbed . . . weary after the great battle" (63, 65) becomes a mournful dirge for fallen heroes. The Ruthwell rune ends at this moment of the poem, it does not continue to Christ's Ascension, nor to the Cross's own rediscovery and raising, its bedecking in gold and silver. The triumphant imagery of the Latinate sides of the Ruthwell Cross—Christ trampling over the Beasts, apostolic feats, and healing miracles—are left to amplify the power of Christ and assert Christianity's presence.[28]

---

[27] Maidie Hilmo, "Visual and Verbal Manifestations of the Dual Nature of Christ on the Ruthwell Cross," in Maidie Hilmo, *Medieval Images, Icons, and Illustrated English Literary Texts: From the Ruthwell Cross to the Ellesmere Chaucer* (Burlington: Ashgate, 2004), 47, likens this stance to that of the warriors in the Anglo-Saxon poem, *The Battle of Maldon.*

[28] Meyer Schapiro provides an interpretation of the imagery of the

The ontological flow between Christ and the Cross is not just anthropomorphism in the service of metaphor. The anthropomorphism of the Cross's desire is conditioned by *wood's* tendency, by what the hewn (not just what the human) wants. As the Cross insists on staying upright, wood's lignin strains to the vertical in the stretch from roots to leaves; as the Cross is slaked and drenched by the blood of Christ, wood's cellulose fibers absorb and transport penetrating fluids.[29] The character of its originary tree remains vibrant and formative in the wood of the Cross. Wrenched from the forest's edge, the tree whose wood will become the Cross carries its primordial tendency with it, and the solidity and upward strain of the tree/the wood/the Cross will bear Christ.[30] The hewn takes over for the human (we see ourselves in broken things), and shapes it with sympathy. Wood's materiality is primal: in language it is at the root of our conceptualization of matter. In Latin, *materia*, the source of our word "matter," starts out meaning "timber."[31] Exploring Isidore of Seville's 7th-century etymology of the word "matter," Caroline Walker Bynum points out its inclusion in a larger discussion of wood and woodworkers, wherein Isidore will claim that matter is "always accepting with regard to something."[32] This "acceptance" is wood's pliability to become table, house, door, gate, cross.

Wood's ability to fluctuate ontologically (to be tree, to be plank, to be cross) manifests itself in artist Melanie Hoff's work, *15,000 Volts*, in which she released 15,000 volts of electricity into a piece of plywood pierced with nails (Figs. 4 and

cross within the religious and territorial struggles of the Northumbrians and the Angles and Britons: "The Religious Meaning of the Ruthwell Cross," *Art Bulletin* 27.4 (1944): 232–245. See also Éamon Ó Carragáin, "The Ruthwell Crucifixion Poem and Its Iconographic and Liturgical Contexts," *Peritia* 6–7 (1987-88): 1–71.

[29] R. Bruce Hoadley, "Cellular Structure," in *Understanding Wood: A Craftsman's Guide to Wood Technology* (Newtown: The Tauton Press, 2000), 17–23.

[30] Michel Pastoureau, "Introduction à la symbolique medieval du bois," in *L'Arbre: Histoire Naturelle et Symbolique de l'Arbre*, ed. Michel Pastoureau (Paris: Cahiers du Léopard d'Or, 1992), 25–40.

[31] Oxford English Dictionary, Vol. 9, 2nd edn. (Oxford: Clarendon Press, 1991), 479–482. The first definition lays the groundwork for the fascinating intertwining of timber, matter, and meaning: "building material, or timber, hence stuff of which a thing is made" (489).

[32] Bynum, *Christian Materiality*, 231.

5). The resulting images argue for the perception of the hewn; they reveal the capacity of wood to respond.[33]

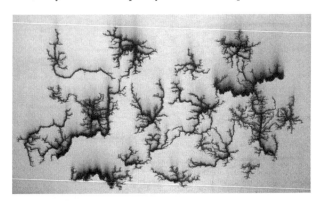

Figure 4. Melanie Hoff, *15,000 Volts*. Electrically treated wood, 2013. Collection of the artist. Printed by permission of the artist.

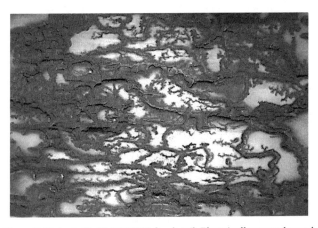

Figure 5. Melanie Hoff, *15,000 Volts*, detail. Electrically treated wood, 2013. Collection of the Artist. Printed by permission of the artist.

[33] See Melanie Hoff's web-page for the artwork (http://melanie-hoff. com/15000volts/) where a time-lapse video reveals the effects of the electricity as it courses through wood. I wish to thank the artist for her gracious permission to use images from various stages of *15,000 Volts*, as well as her generous personal communications with me.

As the electricity courses through the wood panel, it finds its way along the fibers, seeking and pushing openings through which to travel and quicken. As it does, tiny tendrils branch out and, having expanded, begin to connect to each other. The tree's qualities, its fibers and organic vulnerability, guide it to create images of what look like trees and branches. Its primal ontology as wood perpetuates its self-representation as tree. The damage to the wood's physical integrity caused by the electricity becomes the wood's creative act. It uncovers a surprising self-portrait in an arboreal vein, as the wood of the Cross is revealed to itself as *the* Cross once it has been pierced by nails and drenched in blood. Damage, then, or what humans would call suffering, becomes part of the self-revelation of the hewn. The human response to this ecological interaction of electricity and wood insists on the element of suffering: the slow scorching of the pale surface looks painful, the pervasive burning, once the electricity has had its way within the wood, leaves a finely etched surface of scars. *15,000 Volts* shifts the temporal scale of suffering: the perceptual time of suffering of the human is brief compared to that of the arboreal—a human life compared to a lifetime in a forest. As the *Dream of the Rood* invites a human meditation on the temporal terms of the tree (becoming Cross, enduring Crucifixion, buried and forgotten to resurge as bedecked Crucifix), so, too, *15,000 volts*, in compressing eight hours of filming into two and a half minutes of video images, converges human and arboreal temporal scales. Yes, we anthropomorphize the wood as we imagine its suffering through the coursing of 15,000 volts. But the wood also arboreomorphizes the human: its cellulose fibers revealed by the electricity into a pattern of veins, its surface like a pale skin. The Cross's heroics project and display Christ's own.

Few hewn things are able to express the transition from whole to hewn within a subjectivity articulated so insistently on sensation and materiality the way the Cross can in the *Dream of the Rood*. The Cross's consciousness of its own ontological shifts from tree to wood to cross simultaneously preserve its sameness (its character as a tree activates its sensations as a cross) and perpetuate its differences (it becomes a warrior like Christ only once it is a cross, it will become a bejeweled reliquary in the hands of men). The Cross tends to the heroic, because wood tends to be steadfast. This tendency becomes an intention in the ecology of the inhuman: what the thing tends to do (take root, branch out) becomes its intention (to be steadfast, to multiply). As ever, it operates with and against human intention. The Cross speaks within the Anglo-Saxon poem to an author asleep, a human consciousness eclipsed by the bright light of a dream vision, to make way for the trials and triumphs of the thing. The Cross recounts exactly how it came to be hewn. "That was very long ago, I remember it still, that I was cut down from the edge of the wood" (28–29). The tree's marginal position, at the forest's edge, had already exposed it to the world of men. In the *Dream of the Rood*, the Cross does not just have consciousness, desire, and suffering: it also has memory. It remembers its place at the edge of the wood, the ripping of its roots when the men came, the strength of the shoulders that carried it up upon the hill and "fastened me there" (33).

Figure 6. Ceremonial Cross of Countess Gertrude. 1038 or shortly after. Germany, Lower Saxony? Gold: worked in repoussé; cloisonné enamel, intaglio, gems, pearls, wood core. 24.2 x 21.6 cm. Purchase from the J.H. Wade Fund with the addition of a gift from Mrs. Edward B. Greene. 1931.55. Printed with permission of the Cleveland Museum of Art.

The hewn *tends* to remember its origin, but makes no pretense of going back. The ecology of the inhuman perpetuates itself to the next cutting; it is only the human that yearns to return to Eden. At the halfway point of her time-lapse recording of wood's endurance of 15,000 volts of electricity, the artist Melanie Hoff reverses the film, erasing the fractal marks of electricity. To my human perception, this reversal seeks to erase suffering, retracing a path to a painless pristine state, and I watch in relief as the fibers singed apart to create tree-like patterns recede into the wholeness of the wood. The wood, however, does not need a return to survive (the Cross remembers its place in the forest, but has no desire to return to it). The wood's suffering, its mutilation, has, like the Cross, transformed it into a work of art: a wooden panel into which a fractal landscape of tree forms has been etched by the wood's conduit of electricity; a bejeweled cross whose wooden core supports gleaming ornament and shimmering surface. Humans watch in fascination as the inhuman becomes its own thing after suffering at their hands. The Cross revels in its recuperation, it rejoices when, after being buried, "friends discovered me there, and adorned me with gold and silver" (76).[34] Wood persists and, in the sacramental treatment of the hewn arguably amplifies, in the complex ontology of ceremonial crosses such as that of Countess Gertrude (Fig. 6), whose gold and silver adornments, and crystal and gem ornamentation, simultaneously obscure and valorize a wooden core that recalls the primeval wood of the Cross. The hewn is creative and generative; its severance from a lost original creating adherences in perpetuity. But that resonant wooden core is a human desire. The hewn doesn't seek a return to Eden—it's the ecology of the *human* that is nostalgic, that yearns to efface. The ecology of the inhuman as manifested in the hewn, as much as it remembers its origin, is always forever cut off, it is always forever moving towards its next assemblage. The wood of the Cross always strives towards its next hewing, the next cut, the next relic.

---

[34] Verses of the *Dream of the Rood* are also found on the gold and silver cross reliquary known as the Brussels Cross, now stripped of its gems, but still displaying its *Rood* inscriptions. See S.T.R.O. d'Ardenne, "The Old English Inscription on the Brussels Cross," *English Studies* 21 (1939): 145–164.

Hewn Redux

Figure 7. The Angel Giving Seth the Branch. Hours of Catherine of Cleves (M. 917/945), Vol. 1, p. 85, Utrecht, the Netherlands, ca. 1440. The Pierpoint Morgan Library, New York. Purchased on the Belle da Costa Greene Fund ad with the assistance of the Fellows, 1963. Printed with the permission of the Pierpont Morgan Library.

Through Adam's desire and Seth's filial courage, the 13th-century "Legend of the Holy Wood" claims the origins of the wood of the Cross in Eden.[35] As Adam lies dying, he yearns for Eden, and Seth is sent to the garden to retrieve and re-

[35] Jacobus de Voragine, "The Invention of the Holy Cross (May 3)," in *The Golden Legend: Reading on the Saints*, trans. William Granger Ryan (Princeton: Princeton University Press, 2012), 277.

claim just a tiny piece of Paradise, oil from the Tree of Mercy in some versions, a branch from the Tree of Knowledge in others.[36] He finds his way back to Eden by following his parents' footprints, burned into the ground by their sorrow when they left it (Fig. 7). It is an incredible journey to make, fervent in its desire for return and restoration, poignant in its ambition born of loss, tragic in its gambit to be hewn and whole. Christian typology amplifies Seth's hewing: the branch that Seth brings back from Eden and plants over his father's grave takes root and will become the tree from which the wood of the cross of Christ's Crucifixion will be cut.[37]

Seth is the only one to take something out of Eden. A hewster nearing Paradise, compelled by his dying father's yearning, he takes from the Garden itself.[38] When he approaches the towering, guarded walls of Eden in the 15th-century Hours of Catherine of Cleves, Seth does so as a pilgrim, walking staff and hat in hand, shoulders hunched beneath a cloak, legs clad in sturdy boots. He approaches this holy land as one well worn in the ways of the world. The Archangel Michael hands him a flowering branch at the threshold of Paradise. A complete return is impossible: Seth will never walk within the Garden, nor feel its perfumed air envelop him; he will never taste of its fruits, nor press against its trees. But he can be given a branch hewn from the Tree of Knowledge, the very thing that will simultaneously perpetuate humanity's nostalgia for a return to Paradise Lost, while proliferating itself along an ontological trajectory of no return. The wood of the Cross never looks back: it will be found

[36] Christian literature about Seth is shaped by the Jewish texts *Vita Adae et Evae* and the Apocalypse of Moses; see A.F.J. Klijn, *Seth in Jewish, Christian, and Gnostic Literature* (Leiden, E.J. Brill, 1977).

[37] Christian typology of the wood of the tree of Eden as the wood of the tree of the Cross begins in the 12th century in the work of Honorius of Autun, and is disseminated in the popular 13th-cenutry text of the Golden Legend. For the fascinating trajectory from typological mention to stand-alone narrative within Christianity, see Barbara Baert, "From Paradise to Golgotha: The Legend of the Wood of the Cross," in *A Heritage of Holy Wood: The Legend of the True Cross in Text and Image*, trans. Lee Preedy (Leiden: Brill, 2004), 289–349.

[38] I am working here with the version of the narrative that prizes Seth's taking of a branch from the Tree of Knowledge. For this and other version articulated in the Middle Ages, involving the oil of the tree of mercy among others, see Esther Casier Quinn, *The Quest of Seth for the Oil of Life* (Chicago: University of Chicago, 1962).

by Solomon and confound him when he cannot make it fit into the construction of his Temple; it will be revered by Sheba when she recognizes it as holy; it will be buried and uncovered within a pool, to be made into the Cross upon which Christ will be crucified. And then, hewn and re-hewn multiple times, it will call out to the human, compel its own representation and adornment, and exist in multiple manifestations materialized in stone, words, gems, signs, and so many other things. The hewn resists erasure and return; it embraces trajectory and accretion, it forever regenerates, bedecked and bejeweled by the hewster.

HUMAN

Alan Montroso

Object-oriented ontology (OOO) insists that in this thick, swirling mess of the capricious and the immutable, the tangible and the unfathomable, the obvious and the occult, all objects share the same ontological status; all objects are *real*.[1] An object is at once its aesthetic qualities, its relationality and affective being as it forms relations with the world, and a withdrawn core that is inaccessible even to the object itself. In order to move beyond the limits of humanism and anthropocentric thinking which plagues philosophic inquiry, object-oriented ontologists often forgo speaking about humans and focus instead on all the other *things* that make up

---

[1] Levi Bryant calls this shared ontological status a "flat ontology," borrowing the term from Manual De Landa. For more on Bryant's expanded notion of flat ontology, see his book *The Democracy of Objects* (Ann Arbor: Open Humanities Press/MPublishing, 2011), as well as his chapter "The Ontic Principle: Outline of an Object-Oriented Ontology," in *The Speculative Turn: Continental Materialism and Realism*, eds. Levi Bryant, Nick Srnicek and Graham Harman (Melbourne: re.press), 261–278.

the networks and assemblages of reality. Yet, in a move quite rare for the literature of OOO, Graham Harman pauses to reflect on the nature of real objects using a human, American philosopher Richard Rorty, as example:

> In the spirit of fun, and to emphasize the point further, it might be noted that even *Richard Rorty himself* is simultaneously present-at-hand and ready-to-hand. . . . Rorty *exists as a reality.* The world would be a different place if he did not exist: different for his vast network of readers, colleagues, family, friends, and even for the Charlottesville and Palo Alto merchants from whom he must have purchased thousands of goods over the years. Nor can the being of Richard Rorty be regarded as something subjective or internal in a mental sense, a being to which he would have direct or privileged access. If his know-ledge of Rorty is better than ours, this difference is still only a matter of degree, not an ontological gulf. Rorty is presumably just as vulnerable as the rest of us to stunning self-discoveries and unexplained physical pains that arise from out of nowhere.[2]

Harman concludes from this that all objects possess both a set of expected utilities as well as other virtual powers that may arise unexpectedly, and that the object emerges from the rift between these ready-to-hand and present-at-hand qualities. [3]This move, which uses a human to illustrate the nature of *all* real objects, is at least as effective for undermining the discourses founded upon human epistemology as simply not speaking about humans at all, since it invites us to reconsider the human as just another object, another thing that shares an equal ontological status with all other things and is therefore subject to the same measure of philosophical scrutiny as a sauce pan or a soliloquy. Which is also to say: we need to elevate inanimate objects to the same status within the multiplicity of discursive contexts that is normally reserved for the human, instead of always objectifying non-human things.[4]

---

[2] Graham Harman, *Tool Being: Heidegger and the Metaphysics of Objects* (Chicago: Open Court Publishing Company, 2002), 167.

[3] Harman, *Tool Being*, 167.

[4] Describing the potential of OOO to engage in feminist conversations about objectification, Graham Harman writes on his blog: "Objectification=reductionism. By contrast, object-oriented ontology is

In an attempt to follow Harman's lead and think about humans as real objects and not privileged subjects, this essay examines the various ways that noises in Chaucer's *Prioress's Tale* engage, influence and commit violence upon the human characters in their various efforts to manifest and sustain their sonic *beingness*. Music is an actant, an ontologically *real*, sonic body that forms relations by means of its own unique agency, creating a musico-human assemblage. I read the *Prioress's Tale* alongside Michel Serres's notions of noise and the parasite, Deleuze & Guattari's sense of the refrain, and Jacques Attali's sociopolitical investigations of music, as well as various perspectives within OOO, to illustrate the way that sounds swell and spread like viruses as they manipulate human hosts in their struggle for sustenance and proliferation.

Through the formulation of a literary praxis of OOO's theory, this essay offers a response to Ian Bogost's invitation in *Alien Phenomenology* to encounter the material world from the perspective of non-human units and investigate what other objects perceive when they interact with and engage humans.[5] Although it is impossible to ever *know* the subjective experience of another being, to sense what an undulating wave senses or to perceive what a gamma ray perceives, these acts of sensation and perception are them-

an anti-reductionist philosophy. It holds that all things must be taken on their own terms. The reason for complaints about "objectification" is that a false split is made between people and maybe animals who *cannot* be objectified, and inanimate objects which *can*. My thesis, by contrast, is that even inanimate objects should not and cannot be objectified. It's not about 'reducing people to objects,' but about raising the status of objects to the level of people": "Levi on Reid-Bowen on feminism and OOO," *Object-oriented Philosophy*, January 22, 2010: doctorzamalek2.wordpress.com/2010/01/22/levi-on-reid-bowen-on-feminism-and-ooo/.

[5] Ian Bogost, *Alien Phenomenology, or What It's Like to Be a Thing* (Minneapolis: University of Minnesota Press, 2012). Bogost proposes a process called "carpentry," by which he implores philosophers to investigate materiality by actually engaging with matter in hands-on approaches in lieu of simply writing about it; "carpentry entails making things that explain how things make their world"(93). Although the sheer fact that this is an essay stands in opposition to Bogost's fundamental assertion that carpentry means engaging with objects and not words, by choosing as my subject matter the world-making performed by two very real entities, it is my hope that this essay acts as a blueprint which describes the construction of a musico-human instrument and proves me to be a skilled carpenter.

selves unique objects that we can worry over and that tell us more about the unique experiences of objects, the ways that *things* put humans to use. As Bogost states, "The experiences of things can be characterized only by tracing the exhaust of their effects on the surrounding world and speculating about the coupling between that black noise and the experience internal to an object"[6]. By navigating the "black noise" produced by the relationship between musical and human objects in *The Prioress's Tale*, the violence a hymn can inflict on other bodies in its attempt to generate and re-generate its very being, noise reveals the ways in which it *parasites* humans.

VIRUS

Jacques Attali, in his Marxist reading of noise as the prophetic harbinger of new economic orders, defines music as "noise given form according to a code . . . that is theoretically knowable by the listener."[7] He is careful to assert, however, that "music cannot be equated with a language," and that music "has neither meaning nor finality."[8] Music, then, is extra-linguistic, for a song *may* be inscribed with a code, a set of lyrics, perhaps. This code, however, emerges from the song as the hope of the inscriber, the lyricist's desire for a body which will make sense of the code, and although the song may be the mediator of the code, it does not rely solely on this lexical content in order to flourish. Or, to put it another way, music *may* be imbricated in human sociopolitical networks, but as a withdrawn object it is only partially revealed to the humans with which it may engage and is just as likely to relate to other objects in ways unrecognizable by our limited cognitive resources.

The musical object resonates harmoniously with what Deleuze and Guattari refer to as the refrain in *A Thousand Plateaus*. They argue that rhythm is the first congealing of chaos into order, not an ordered being itself but a passing-into order, a making-home, the establishing of a relation to the other and to itself; "the song itself is already a skip: it jumps from chaos to the beginnings of order in chaos and is

---

[6] Bogost, *Alien Phenomenology*, 100.

[7] Jacques Attali, *Noise: A Political Economy of Music*, trans. Brian Massumu (Minneapolis: University of Minnesota, 1985), 25.

[8] Attali, *Noise*, 25.

in danger of breaking apart at any moment."[9] Rhythm is temporality, or the possibility of temporality, and the refrain, territoriality and immanence, space-making, an ordered moment in the perpetual chaos of material reality. And as the preponderance of verbs in the quote above suggest, it also is a self-replicating order, a transmission of moments, which effect their own space-making gesture.

Deleuze and Guattari use birdsong to illustrate this process of territorialization-from-chaos. When the bird sings in response to its milieu, say the rising of the sun, the bird organizes the event, the arrival of chaotic solar energy by means of its own avian mode of being in the world. When it produces a harmony in response to this natural event, it in effect translates the dawn into an expression of birdness, a sonic gesture that makes sense of chaos through the organizing principal of the avian melody. This harmony creates a space of relationality for birds of the same species, a refrain that thereby establishes an identity, a community, through its iterative performance. Of course, no act of territorialization is permanent or immutable, and the birdsong always produces a surplus capable of disrupting the stability of the system, opening a space for re-territorialization: "the territory already unleashes something that will surpass it."[10] For birdsong, once manifest, becomes its own unique object, which directs its own agency; the refrain is capable of not only being corrupted or de-territorialized, but itself might re-territorialize or corrupt other objects.

Music emerges from its instrument as flies into the world as an object, a *real* object, intangible and evanescent, perhaps, but real nonetheless. The sonic object, the refrain, a song, rhythm itself, is a haecceity[11] which interrupts the

[9] Gilles Deleuze and Félix Guattari, *A Thousand Plateaus: Capitalism and Schizophrenia*, trans. Brian Massumi (Minneapolis: University of Minnesota Press, 1987), 311.

[10] Deleuze and Guattari, *A Thousand Plateaus*, 322. Interestingly, Deleuze and Guattari cite an example of a parasitic species of bird, the *Viduinae*, that adopts its courtship song from the host, thus re-territorializing another bird's song; or, from the perspective of the song itself, the Viduina is parasited by the harmony made manifest by the host bird. See note 37 to "1837: Of the Refrain" (550).

[11] The medieval theologian and philosopher Duns Scotus first proposed the term haecceity, or "thisness," to emphasize the positive, unique, discrete presence of a thing, the intrinsic being of an object, distinct from its qualities, that makes it indivisible and individual. See Scotus, *Ordinatio* II d.3 p.1 q. 2, as well as q. 4. The Peter King

flows and relations of other objects to satisfy its indelible need to perpetuate, to radiate its materiality and to engage in causal relations with other objects. Music is only coded noise when it engages with particular types of objects like humans or birds, which are sensitive to codes, which perceive and/or produce semiotic systems. If song is "in danger of breaking apart at any moment," that is because it is born of relations, it is an object bred from the marriages of other objects as they mingle and mate on an aesthetic level, at the level of appearances. The sonic event is a radiation that occurs between objects, between two or more withdrawn entities that can only strive to touch each other aesthetically, metaphorically.[12]

Thus a song, such as a Marian hymn, is a virus, born of and in the relations of directionless and atemporal objects when they attempt to congeal in the spaces they create and the times they, well, *time*.[13] Object-oriented ontology reminds us that objects are at once entirely concealed from even themselves and simultaneously always bathing in a sea of sensual qualities, making manifest their own space and their own time *as* they emerge, giving shape to reality and not just acting within it as if reality were some distinct fluid or net within which all objects struggle and play. Music manifests its agency through its aesthetic qualities because it is only by means of these sensual features that withdrawn objects communicate, correspond, touch. In its ephemeral and capricious dance of sensual virtues, then, the sonic event can arrive as either a mellifluous, if somewhat impetuous, being with an appetite for transmission, or an arrhythmic, discordant relation that parasites other harmonies.

translations are available from the Franciscan Archive: http://www.franciscan-archive.org/scotus/index.html#writings.

[12] Timothy Morton argues that, since objects only make sense of each other via their own sensual qualities, the real essence of the objects always remaining withdrawn, then causality is a purely aesthetic phenomena. Objects must translate each other in terms of their own sense-making apparatuses, much like the work of the metaphor in poetry. See, for instance "An Object-Oriented Defense of Poetry," *New Literary History* 43.2 (Spring 2012): 205–224.

[13] I give credit to Morton for my use of "time" as a verb. He writes, "Objects are not 'in' time and space. Rather, they 'time' (a verb) and 'space'": "Objects as Temporary Autonomous Zones," *continent.* 1.3 (2011): 152 [149–155].

BIOSYNTHESIS

Michel Serres describes the parasite as an uninvited guest enjoying the labors of a host who did not plan to play the host, as well as, from the French "les parasites," static, noise that alters the state of things by interrupting trajectories and reorienting relationships.[14] In Chaucer's *Prioress's Tale*, just such a parasite exists—a parasitic song. The *Prioress's Tale* is the curiously brutal and complicatedly anti-Semitic narrative in which a young Christian child is murdered and dumped in a privy by Jews for his singing of the Marian antiphon, *Alma Redemptoris Mater*, and yet whose body continues to sing post-mortem.[15] What happens if, instead of focusing on the too-human violence of the narrative, we look instead from the perspective of music itself, if we look at the particular iteration of music, the *Alma Redemptoris* hymn, as a autopoietic agent that works to perpetuate its own existence regardless of the condition of the material within which it finds itself embodied? Perhaps we can supplement readings that get mired in the text's execrable violence and flagrant anti-Semitism if we study the tool-being, the instrumentality of the child's sonorous body from the perspective of song.

The *Prioress's Tale* is itself a musical body, being one of only four from *The Canterbury Tales* to be composed in the formal stanzas known as Rhyme Royal. Although the Rhyme Royal form works to emphasize the moral seriousness of

---

[14] Michel Serres, *The Parasite*, trans. Lawrence R. Schehr (Minneapolis: University of Minnesota Press, 2007). Serres uses the fable of the city rat and the country rat to illustrate the shifting nature of the guest/host relationship, with the introduction of the farmer's noise which chases the rats away from their meal the third-sense of "parasite" as a static which re-orients relationships. "One parasite chases another out. One parasite (static), in the sense that information theory uses the word, chases another, in the anthropological sense" (6).

[15] Anthony Bale rigorously investigates the complicated anti-Jewish sentiment of the *Prioress's Tale* as he reads it alongside a wealth of analogous medieval tales of children executed by Jews for singing Christian hymns in the third chapter of *The Jew and the Medieval Book: English Antisemitisms, 1350-1500* (New York: Cambridge University Press, 2006). Among other things, he convincingly argues that there exists among the texts not a consistent thread of anti-Semitism, but a multiplicity of anti-Semitisms determined by place, political power, economic forces and the tenuous struggle of Christianity to define itself in opposition to Judaism even when differences are not apparent.

those four tales,[16] it is also particularly relevant that the *Prioress's Tale*, oriented as it is around the strange and miraculous efficacy of a hymn, is already a sort of song, a rhythmic series of refrains written to a dulcet cadence that moves and manipulates the reader. In fact, in the prologue, the Prioress actually refers to her tale as "my song" (VII.487).[17] By weaving the iambic pentameter lines into such a harmonious rhyme scheme, the narrative, by way of its agency and affective musicality, lulls the human audience into a sense of comfort and trust. The readers of the tale are infected by its music.

Alma Redemptoris first appears much the way any virus arrives: via contact with a previously infected host. The hymn transmits itself at the child's school, and the "litel clergeon" is distracted from his learning as he overhears the hymn as it erupts from the throats of another class of children learning from their antiphoners.[18] But a song is a bodiless *moving-towards*, pure directionality, and will perish unless it finds another host to infect; thus, like the song of a siren, the *Alma Redemptoris* exerts its self-sustaining agency as it captivates the clergeon and draws him "ner and ner" (VII.520). The instant it graces his ears, the pathogen-like hymn inhabits the child and embeds itself so deep within his memory that he cannot forget the tune, even though "Noght

[16] The other three tales are, of course, the *Second Nun's Tale*, the *Clerk's Tale*, and the *Man of Law's Tale*, in which similar themes of persecution, martyrdom, and Christian devotion are explored.

[17] All quotations from the *Prioress's Tale* are taken from Larry D. Benson, gen. ed., *The Riverside Chaucer*, 3rd edn. (Boston: Houghton Mifflin, 1987), and are cited by fragment and line number.

[18] Bruce Holsinger locates the medieval school as a site of bodily violence in his critically important book, *Music, Body, and Desire in Medieval Culture: Hildegard of Bingen to Chaucer* (Stanford: Stanford University Press, 2001). While I certainly agree with Holsinger's argument that music functions as an apparatus for constituting Christian identity and creating pedagogical subjects by means of its performing as a punitive measure within the medieval education system, his reading nevertheless emerges from an anthropocentric orientation which privileges the human subject and relegates music to the role of tool for effective punishment. Music's real power, according to Holsinger's reading, comes from its symbolic association with threats of physical pain at the hands of the instructor, as well as its being a performative tool for demarcating racial difference. I argue that, in addition to this reading, music *itself* enacts its own very real and very material violence regardless of its symbolic resonance within the human epistemological experience.

wiste he what this Latyn was to seye" (VII.523). It is the sound itself and not any sense or semiotic significance that affects the listener. Even the older boy to whom the clergeon turns in order to learn the linguistic meaning of the hymn, after offering a cursory exegesis, admits, "I lerne song; I kan but small grammeere" (VII.536). The agencies of the hymn, then, are its rhythmic qualities on the aesthetic plane, the cadences it carves out of chaos in order to shape itself; the lyrical content is only a secondary quality, a mnemonic device with which music reinforces its presence and ensures its perpetuation and retransmission.

Once infected, the Prioress's child unwittingly becomes a captive of music's indelible need to manifest and reproduce its own being. The clergeon shares his physical body with the *Alma Redemptoris*; "twies a day it passed thurgh his throte" (VII.548). The Prioress's boy is simultaneously an instrument for the production of music and a host from which the *Alma Redemptoris* continues to replicate. Song must rely on the host/instrument to give shape to its accidental properties, because it is by these properties that the sonic substance is able to parasite relations and continue to spread as an infection. The real sonic event entangles itself with its host, not as an intentional object of the human mind but as a real, yet withdrawn, entity capable of surprising the host by arriving unannounced with the sudden urge to sing.

Serres speaks of the paralytic on the back of the blind man, guiding the blind man so they both might move, immobile information on the shoulders of a source of transportation, bartering information for mobility.[19] The relationship *seems* symbiotic, the union of two objects for their mutual benefit. Nevertheless, the paralytic is a parasite, letting the blind man believe the relationship is balanced, when, in fact, he who rides on the shoulders of another's labor possesses all the information, and thus, all the power; he is the primary operator of this motility-machine. Serres' parable may be intended to allegorize sociopolitical systems of control, governments and economies, but is just as surely serves as an apt metaphor for the relationship between the Prioress's child and the hymn. The *Alma Redemporis* is the crippled object, relying on the organic body's mobility in order to transmit its information, and the "litel clergeon" is its instrument, affected by the hymn in order that it might mani-

---

[19] Serres, *The Parasite*, 35–37.

fest and thereby reproduce the musical virus. The song is the position of power, erupting unexpectedly and controlling the vehicle in order to perpetuate its own *beingness* in the world.

LYSIS

> One parasite chases out the other.
>> Michel Serres, *The Parasite*[20]

Thus music, the hymn, the parasitic object preying on its host, although invisible and evanescent, is a real object carving out its own space, making territory for itself. Deleuze & Guattari say of the territory:

> There is a territory precisely when the milieu components cease to be directional, becoming dimensional instead, when they cease to be functional to become expressive. There is a territory when the rhythm has expressiveness. What defines the territory is the emergence of matters of expression (qualities).[21]

The *Alma Redemptoris Mater*, once it is established inside the host, once its congealing into a coherent refrain is accomplished, evolves into an aesthetic, a song, a rhythm that gets repeated as the child travels about his environment singing enthusiastically. It becomes a dimensional object, its sensual qualities reaching out to the various assemblages of its milieu as it continues to infect.

When the host body carries the song into the Jewry, however, the viral hymn encounters another parasite that seeks to overthrow its position of power over humans:

> Oure firste foo, the serpent Sathanas,
> That hath in Jues herte his wasps nest,
> Up swal, and seide, "O Hebrayk peple, allas!
> Is this to yow a thing that is honest,
> That swich a boy shal walken as hym lest
> In youre despit, and synge of swich sentence,
> Which is again youre laws reverence?"
> (VII.558–564)

The serpent which is Satan incites the Jews to silence the

---

[20] Serres, *The Parasite*, 6.
[21] Deleuze and Guattari, *A Thousand Plateaus*, 315.

infectious song traveling through their alley by snuffing out the life of its host. That Satan is said to be located in a wasps nest in the hearts of the Jews introduces a new sonic being into the narrative, a buzzing sound, static, the interference signified by the French *les parasites.* The Satanic buzzing is a noise, which preys on relations, which feeds on hosts, which rearranges the shape of networks and gives rise to narrative. "That noise too interrupted a process: a trip. And from this noise comes the story. Hosts and parasites are always in the process of passing by, being sent away, touring around, walking alone. They exchange places in a space soon to be defined."[22] The buzzing enters the system and seeks to displace the first parasite, the hymn, the uninvited guest. Serres writes further: "[i]n the system, noise and message exchange roles according to the position of the observer and the action of the actor, but they are transformed into one another as well as a function of time and of the system. They make order or disorder." The hostile buzzing interferes with the original system, delivering a message of violence as it seeks to cast out the parasitic hymn by eradicating its host.

And yet, another exchange of roles occurs here from the perspective of the human hosts themselves; for the hymn is doubly parasitic in the sense that it not only parasites the child, but its Christian code, its explicitly for-human content, destabilizes and even perhaps reverses the expected relationship between Christian and Jew in *The Prioress's Tale.* The tale itself is set in an imaginary city, for Jews had long been expelled from England, and the Prioress must represent a no-place in order to spin her anti-Semitic yarn. This Asian city has as its center a Jewry, which, as Anthony Bale reminds us, is *not* a ghetto, for the act of ghettoizing Jewish communities "is an invention of a later age."[23] The Jewry is the center of commerce, of mercantile exchange, an alley market open at both ends, through which "men myghte ride or wende" (7.493). Bale asserts that, "The Jewry is not a contagious or leaking corrupt body, but rather an entity which is entered by non-Jews . . . Christianity enters, and is lodged within, Jewish space, not *vice versa.*"[24] Although the Prioress qualifies the business of the Jewry as "foule usure and lucre of vileynye," we nevertheless assume that the

[22] Serres, *The Parasite,* 16.
[23] Bale, *The Jew and the Medieval Book,* 64.
[24] Bale, *The Jew and the Medieval Book,* 83.

community at large, its "Cristene folk," benefit greatly from the Jewish "lucre" (VII.491). If so, then it is the Christian populace that parasites the Jews, for as it moves through the Jewry, it reaps profits while sowing only discord and violence. Furthermore, the "litel scole" of the Christian child is located at the end of the alley, and thus seems to invade, or at least belong to, the Jewry. The young boy's singing the Marian hymn, then, can be seen as an attempt to deterritorialize and parasite Jewish space.

In order to demonize the Jews and thereby underscore the moral rectitude of the tale's Christian figures—as well as further justify the Christian colonization of the Jewry the Prioress marks the Jews as parasites, or vectors for a satanic parasite. She creates a bit of noise to not only corrupt the Jews but to conceal the Christian's own culpability and parasitism. Yet this buzzing, this noise's proximity to the apostrophe, "O Hebrayk people," in the passage quoted above already suggests a misapprehension on the part of the Prioress, for referring to the people as Hebrayk conflates the foreign Jewish language with the identity of its speakers. Through this Christian lens, then, the incomprehensible language of an ethno-religious group is metamorphosed into a demonic buzzing and the group itself is rendered susceptible to a satanic parasite. The Prioress's representation of Jews as infected bodies that possess an insectile humming instead of proper human language also reveals her Christian desire to re-territorialize Jewish space, to imagine the Jews as sub- or inhuman parasites in order to more fully justify their horrific extermination. For the Prioress, Jewish hearts must impiously buzz in order that the Marian hymn justifiably supersede the immoral "Hebrayk" noise.

The text's privileging a lyrical song over nonsensical buzzing begs the following question: What is the ontological distinction, if any, between noise and music, between static and song? Perhaps it is only in the thoughts or experiences of the operators that noise and music have different meanings. A thumping bass-beat from a passing car, the notes stretching with the Doppler effect, is perhaps just "noise" to the man sweeping his sidewalk, to the leaves being swept, to the cat under the porch; but surely to the woman driving the car it is music, a song. Perhaps Serres treats music in the chapter called "Noise," but talks about work in the chapter titled "Music" because he recognizes the hazards of too readily distinguishing between the two. The nature of the sonic object, forever withdrawn even from itself, is its relation to relations, and the other objects in the vicinity of sound make determinations about its being only after the arrival and departure of the sonic event by examining the harmonic residue with whatever limited aesthetic capacities those objects possess.

Thus, when Attali, in a formalist move which links music to myth via Levi-Strauss, argues that noise is a simulacrum of the general violence of human nature, and music, then, the ordered ritual sacrifice that channels and redirects human violence, he attends too much to the human notion that music and noise are categorically different objects.[25] The distinction between harmony and cacophony is only a judgment made by a body affected by sound;[26] therefore *every* sonic event carries at least the potential for violence; every sound, from birdsong to bomb-blast, introduces the risk that the relations between objects may be silently and delicately smothered or raucously, rancorously ruptured. Noise, once it has graduated from directionality to dimensionality, must seek to defend its position of power over whatever host it is parasiting, or risk fading from existence.

If, however, Attali is correct in linking sound with violence, we must consider how such an ephemeral, invisible object is capable of manifesting a real, physical assault. A basic principal of object-oriented ontology holds that objects themselves, the real withdrawn cores of various beings, never in fact touch each other; it is only their sensual qualities which engage and interact, and even this only at the level of intention for whichever object is trying to engage another. For Morton, this sensual interaction occurs on the aesthetic plane;[27] Harman describes object relations as vicarious causation,[28] and Bogost clarifies what is occasionally a rather confusing proposition by calling for metaphor and caricature

[25] Attali, *Noise*, 26–31. Further, "Music responds to the terror of noise, recreating differences between sounds and repressing the tragic dimension of lasting dissonance—just as sacrifice responds to the terror of violence" (28).

[26] Which is not to say that the judgment itself doesn't produce real change in the world or alter the relationships between objects, but an unconscious ruling based on the regulations of a semiotic system, likely of human origin, which distinguishes music from noise does not prove any real ontological distinction between the two.

[27] See Morton, "An Object-Oriented Defense of Poetry."

[28] For more on Harman's vicarious causation, see his lush and poetic essay "On Vicarious Causation," in *COLLAPSE*, Vol. II: Speculative Realism, ed. Robin Mackay (Oxford: Urbanomic, 2007) 171–205.

in order to understand the operations between objects.[29] If their language is different, these three are nevertheless theoretically in agreement that all objects manifest sensual qualities which are *distinct* and discretely different than their withdrawn cores, and it is only through relations in the aesthetic realm that things make contact.

Thus music, as an incorporeal object, performs its agency at the aesthetic level, the only level at which all objects are capable of interacting. Noise, here synonymous with music, acts precisely where intentional objects attempt to establish contact with the sensual qualities of other beings by either disrupting or obviating altogether the relation; this is the opulence of music, its parasitism. Returning to Serres,

> To play the position or to play the location is to dominate the relation. It is to have a relation only with the relation itself. Never with the stations from which it comes, to which it goes, and by which it passes. Never to the things as such and, undoubtedly, never to subjects as such. Or rather, to those points as operators, as sources of relations. And this is the meaning of the prefix *para-* in the word *parasite*: it is on the side, next to, shifted; it is not on the thing, but on its relation.[30]

Take this example from Ovid: In book XI of the *Metamorphoses*, we find Orpheus attacked by a roving group of Bacchantes while Orpheus is manipulating trees, creatures and stones by the agency of his song. The Bacchantes' attempts to kill Orpheus by hurling projectiles at him are repeatedly thwarted by the raw force of his music.[31] It is only after the wild women invite noise into their onslaught, both the music

---

[29] For more on Bogost's clarification of OOO's position on relationality, see the chapter "Metaphorism," in *Alien Phenomenology*, 61–84.

[30] Serres, *The Parasite*, 38.

[31] It is worth noting a recent study of granular impact in which the kinetic energy of a grain being dropped into a bed of photoelastic disks (particles that emit light commensurate to the forces acting upon them) is dissipated through its transformation into acoustic energy. Kinetic energy becomes a sonic event; or, sound is responsible for reducing the forces that occur between two objects in contact, just as Orpheus's music buffers him from the forces of the projectiles hurled by the Bacchantes. See Abram H. Clark et al., "Particle Scale Dynamics in Granular Impact," *Physical Review Letters* 109.23 (2012); DOI: 10.1103/PhysRevLett.109.238302.

of trumpets and the ululations of their own voices,[32] that they are able to rupture the relation between Orpheus and his song and finally kill him. The human characters are not inflicting violence on each other as much as the various noises are waging a battle simultaneously physical *and* aesthetic. The subjects in the heat of combat, Orpheus and the Bacchantes, are alternatively parasited by the sonic bodies determining their relationship. Brutality, the lamentable death of Orpheus, is only possible by means of a sensual vicar; it is only in the presence of noise that the human objects are able to inflict injury. Just as we are given in to the enchantment of music, we are simultaneously made victim of its perpetual struggle to dominate the host and colonize relations.

Thus it is by the allure of two sonic objects, a sacred hymn and a satanic buzzing, that the human characters of the *Prioress's Tale* are borne into conflict. When the "litel clergeon" transports the Marian hymn into the Jewry where the song encounters the supposed wasps' nests of Satan, it is the noises themselves that square off as the inherent violence of their withdrawn essences confront each other on the aesthetic plane. It is a battle of wills between two sonic events, with little regard being paid to the status, effects or outcomes their battle will have on the human hosts. This second virus infects the bodies of those as yet uninfected by the *Alma Redemptoris* and drives them to eradicate the competition.

We cannot, however, forgo the *significance* of this violence at the level of human ideology and ethno-religious conflict. For the Jews, re-presented through the tale's anti-Semitic narrator and thus embodying a static that justifies Christianity's parasiting the Jewry, silence the child by slitting his throat, and dump his body in a privy, as if to insure against any possibility that the sonic infection might continue to spread. Bale locates the privy as a common site of anti-Semitic rhetoric in medieval Europe, especially within the tradition of the Christian exemplum.[33] For Bale, the latrine

---

[32] *sed ingens clamor et infracto Berecyntia tibia cornu tympanaque et plausus et Bacchei ululates obstrepuere sono citharae* ["but the huge clamor of the Berecynthian flute of broken horn, and the drums, and the clapping and wailing of the Bacchantes drowned out the music of the lyre"]: Ovid, *Metamorphoses*, XI.15–18, *The Latin Library*: http://www.thelatinlibrary.com/ovid/ovid.met11.shtml. The translation is mine.

[33] See chapter 2, "History: time, nationhood and the Jew of Tewkes-

emphasizes the bodily, the temporal, the failure of the Jew to honor the Sabbath or to ingest the spiritual body of Christ during the Eucharistic mass. "Excretion and the rectal or faecal trope . . . mark an antithetical extreme in the chain of signifiers within the discourses of incorporation surrounding the Eucharist and Christ's body."[34] Yet moral exempla such as tales of the Jew of Tewkesbury mark the Jewish body as a signifier of Christian curiosity, the potential errantry of all mortal men, and thereby an unstable sign; "the Jew exists . . . in an intimate and mutable relationship with Christianity."[35] Thus the cess-pit becomes a site for emptying anti-Semitic signifiers of their meaning.

If the latrine in *The Prioress's Tale* is thought to protect the Jewish community from the perceived threat of the Christian virus—a virus contracted in a school, no less—then the text also suggests a reversal of its terms, the threat of a sonic contagion an unholy inversion of the Christian's own fear of the "Hebrayk" virus. For a latrine, a pit for human fecal waste, is a *site* of infection, as well as a quarantine, and the tension between these two significances emphasizes the text's anxiety about the position of the Jews in this mutually parasitic relation; who is infecting whom? And how? The Jews fear sacred music and conceal its instrument in a pit of excrement *just as* the good Christian people ought to fear and expel the noise of Satanic temptation to usury, noise borne from a Jewish privy. The human codes conveyed by these sonic objects, then, engender an exemplum for the Christian reader, an exemplum that, by means of its operating through a reversal of terms that provokes a necessary identification *with* the Jews, destabilizes any securely anti-Semitic meaning.

ADAPTATION

> Noise destroys and horrifies. But order and flat repetition are in the vicinity of death. Noise nourishes a new order. Organization, life, and intelligent thought live between order and noise, between disorder and perfect harmony.
>
> Michel Serres, *The Parasite*

A hymn, ephemeral and infectious, will not long be silenced,

bury," in Bale, *The Jew in the Medieval Book*, 23–54.

[34] Bale, *The Jew in the Medieval Book*, 39.

[35] Bale, *The Jew in the Medieval Book*, 43.

and as the mother of the "litel clergeon" searches for the body of her child, the corpse begins to sing once more. The Christian folk of the city wonder at this seemingly miraculous event, that the human body should perform in such an unexpected, impossible manner. Yet, from the perspective of the hymn, driven by its desire for endurance, dimensionality, and the continued spread of the sonic virus, the mortal status of the host is of little concern, so long as it can be made to sing; a broken string, a battered trumpet, or a severed throat may affect the aesthetic qualities of a noise, but so long as the instrument can produce a sound, the sonic parasite will continue to manipulate its host. Thus, when the body "with throte ykorven lay upright, / He *Alma redemptoris* gan to synge / So loude that al the place gan to rynge" (VII.611–613), the "litel clergeon" is simply reprising its role as host for the production of the hymn; it is now only a mere shell of a human, the residue of a child performing its full *being* as a musical instrument and sonorous body.

The human has thus become ready-to-hand in relation to the song, and the child's voice becomes an incorporeal tool for the sake of the hymn. When we investigate the coupling of the parasite and host, we encounter the Prioress's child as a chimera, a creature at once part human and part music. "The musical voice itself becomes-child at the same time as the child becomes sonorous, purely sonorous."[36] The song is not so much "embodied" within a human frame, but completely enmeshed with the organs and relations of a musico-human assemblage. To the human characters, the lifeless child is a miraculously resurrected corpse, but to the Marian hymn, it is an able and resonant instrument, its voice an ephemeral and affective becoming within which human and music coexist.

Timothy Morton refers to this coexistence, the sticky web in which all beings are discrete yet connected, as a "mesh."[37] The notion of a mesh adds dimensionality to Levi Bryant's flat ontology, suggesting that not only do all objects share the same ontological status, but that objects weave in and out of sometimes swirling, sometimes stagnant networks, occasionally overlapping or touching in unpredictable ways. Being so interconnected, enmeshed, means that all objects are

---

[36] Deleuze and Guattari, *A Thousand Plateaus*, 304.
[37] Timothy Morton, *The Ecological Thought* (Cambridge: Harvard University Press, 2010), 28.

more *and* less than what they seem. "The mesh of interconnected things is vast, perhaps immeasurably so. Each entity in the mesh looks strange. Nothing exists all by itself, and so nothing is fully 'itself.'"[38] The mesh is made of objects sentient and insentient, measurable and immeasurable, bursting with vitality and eerily undead. In a mesh, an ephemeral, gossamer object such as a song can nestle up against or inside a spiritless carbon-based life form and jostle it into a seeming animation.

Figure 1: Odelon Redon (French; 1840-1916), *Orpheus*, c. 1903-1910, Cleveland Museum of Art, Cleveland, Ohio.

Returning to Ovid's tale of Orpheus, we find an example of such an entanglement in a scene only too similar to the events of the *Prioress's Tale*. After the Bacchantes murder Orpheus to halt his song, they hew and strew the body parts, the head and lyre abandoned to the river Hebrus. While floating down the river, the song entangles itself once more with the lyre and a lifeless head: *et (mirum!) medio dum labi-*

---

[38] Morton, *The Ecological Thought*, 15.

tur amne, flebile nescio quid queritur lyra, flebile lingua murmurat exanimis, respondent flebile ripae ["and (a miracle!) while gliding down the middle of the river, the lyre lamented mournfully I don't know what, the dead tongue murmured mournfully, mournfully the riverbanks replied"].[39]

Music is the thread uniting this tangled web of grief, performing its agency in objects which we believe to be voiceless (even the lyre needs the application of stress to its strings before it will divulge its hermetic melodies), animating that which we assume to be lifeless. Although we know they are only mingling on the aesthetic plane, at the sensual level, these unexpected manifest sensations evidence the sheer thickness of the mesh of things. For though human perception is limited and we cannot know ("nescio") the inner lives of things, if we attend to objects carefully enough, we may yet get to observe the unexpected and listen to the murmuring ("murmurat") of the inhuman.

By investigating the human from the position of music, we find ourselves with an increasingly more capacious understanding of the human object. We find the corpse of the Prioress's child, like the head of Orpheus, behaving in unexpected ways, shocking us with actions we hardly consider possible for humans to perform. In an enmeshed existence, in which all things overlap and engage each other by means of their own unique sensual qualities, we must realize that what we think of as "human" is surely not the same thing another object experiences as the same object. "Being a person means never being sure that you're one."[40] "One" here can be both a predicate nominative as well as the number one, a single, finite being. Enmeshed objects form compound objects, form strange assemblages and perform novel, mysterious and often inexplicable actions. The experiences of an object cannot be characterized by the sensual or accidental qualities of that object alone.

The revelation of the resurrected corpse, then, is the surprise of the withdrawn being to itself, the bubbling to the surface, by means of a relation to other objects, of unforeseen possibility. For is it not by means of a peculiar relationality to another material object, that hotly disputed "greyn,"

---

[39] Ovid, *Metamorphoses*, XI.51–53, *The Latin Library*: http://www.thelatinlibrary.com/ovid/ovid-met11.shtml. The translation is mine.
[40] Morton, *The Ecological Thought*, 8.

that the human body performs in this most unusual of manners, as a reinvigorated corpse? Even if divine will or Marian grace temporarily revives the dead child, it is only by means of a very real and material vector that a miracle is performed. Whether the Prioress intends a Eucharistic host or a literal seed or bit of wheat, she cannot escape a wondering at the agency and unpredictability of *things*. Her undead singer is an assemblage of human, grain and hymn, a concatenation of object-relations manifesting the marvelous. It is an example of what Ian Bogost refers to as carpentry,[41] a jostling together of objects in a way that invites unexpected interactions between the things involved. By investigating the construction of this musico-granular-human assemblage from the metaphorical vantage of a caricatured sonic object or a kernel of wheat, we find ourselves to be as strange and strangely unpredictable as all other objects in the cosmos. Timothy Morton refers to this unpredictability when he writes of the "strange stranger," a phrase he uses to replace the word "animal" as well as "human." The closer we get to the strange stranger, the more we hone our gaze as we trace its contours and probe its recesses, the more bizarre it becomes. "Far from gradually erasing strangeness, intimacy heightens it. The more we know them, the stranger they become. Intimacy is itself strange."[42] It is within this strange intimacy that non-human objects are capable of temporarily revivifying the dead.

PROLIFERATION

Within the mise-en-scene of human drama and ethno-religious violence that concludes the *Prioress's Tale*, the *Alma Redemptoris Mater* simply persists; it retains its host body and perpetuates its being, still germinating, still infecting and affecting host and audience alike. The subjective experience of the hymn is the ceaseless searching of an incorporeal object for body and form, some instrument from which to manifest its sound, anything capable of producing its melo-

---

[41] Ian Bogost describes carpentry as the philosophically investigative act of working with real objects and bringing objects together in ways that let *things* illustrate the changes they make upon each other and the world. Bogost writes, "carpentry entails making things that explain how things make their world" (*Alien Phenomenology*, 93).

[42] Morton, *The Ecological Thought*, 41.

dy, anything which resonates or reverberates, moving like a plague which hungers only for perpetuity and transmission. A song makes no distinction between life and death, nor does it care for boundaries between the animate and the inanimate, but navigates and operates in the liminal spaces between: thus the severed head of Ovid's Orpheus becomes a vocal instrument, a microphone for a mourning song. For music, a cadaver is a useful tool, a potential sire; music finds life in death, just as the *Alma Redemptoris* perpetuates itself through the "ycorven" throat of a child's corpse in the *Prioress's Tale*.

MATTER

Valerie Allen

For fourteenth-century translator and encyclopedist John Trevisa what characterizes material existence is its measurability. He opens his chapter on measurement thus:

> Mesure, he seiþ, is al þing þat hath ende in wight and lengþe, and in brede, in highnesse, in depnesse, and in oughte. And so oure grete made and mesured al þe wyde world; . . . And so by here witte and sleighte þey lefte noþing vnmesured, from þe moste to þe leste.[1]

> [Measure, he says, is everything that has limits in weight and length, and in breadth, in height, in depth, and anything (like that). And thus our forebears prepared and measured the whole wide world; . . . And so by their knowledge and ingenuity they left nothing unmeasured from the greatest to the least.]

[1] John Trevisa, *On the Properties of Things: John Trevisa's Translation*

Starting with the largest unit imaginable (a Roman province), Trevisa proceeds to the tiny inch, freely mixing area and length as he enumerates. Measurability is the mark of creation, for as the book of wisdom says: "Þu haste imade alle in nombre, wighte, and mesure."[2]

It is telling that many of the measures should be of Roman imperial origin because mastery so often is measurement's motive. For Trevisa, however, mensuration exceeds dominion's intent to establish the fundamental conditions of knowing the material world. Not reliant on conventional language acquisition, counting enables description, representation, and knowledge.[3]

> And noþing we may knowe and conne wiþoute lore of nombres. . . . Take away, he seiþ, noumbre and tale, and alle þinges beþ ylost. Do awey compot and acountes, and al is ful of lewednesse and vnconnynge.[4]

> [And there is nothing we can know and understand without the art of counting. . . . Take away number and measurement, and all is lost. Do away with calculation and account, and everything lapses into worthlessness and ignorance.]

This long-standing association between matter and measurement rests on the assumption that matter is massy and sensorily ascertainable, an assumption that perforce has been reconceptualized in a quantum universe.[5] A "new materialism" challenges the equation between measurability and matter, arguing instead for the latter's vagabond quality, intensity and vibrancy, resistance to calculation, presence beyond representation, and for an agency ordinarily attributed to human action and consciousness.[6] Underlying

[2] Trevisa, *On the Properties of Things*, 1353.

[3] For ways of counting without numbers, see Georges Ifrah, *The Universal History of Numbers: From Prehistory to the Invention of the Computer*, trans. David Bellos et al. (New York: John Wiley, 2000), 3–22.

[4] Trevisa, *On the Properties of Things*, 1354.

[5] See Karen Barad, *Meeting the Universe Halfway: Quantum Physics and the Entanglement of Matter and Meaning* (Durham: Duke University Press, 2007) and her interview in Rick Dolphijn and Iris van der Tuin, eds., *New Materialism: Interviews and Cartographies* (Ann Arbor: Open Humanities Press/MPublishing, 2012), 48–70.

[6] For example, Jane Bennett, *Vibrant Matter: A Political Ecology of*

this investigation into inhuman life is the challenge posed to the philosophical position, classically articulated in Immanuel Kant's transcendentalism, that the material world can be made meaningful only when the light of human consciousness shines on it, that "thought cannot get *outside itself* in order to compare the world as it is 'in itself' to the world as it is 'for us.'"[7]

Pace new materialism's resistance to the temptations of the tape measure, I pursue the kindred relation between calculation and matter in this essay to note that measurement is no self-evident exercise and propose that its representations speculate as well as and maybe better than metaphor. The very terms that have become the metaphors of new materialism—networks, entanglement, flow, fields, lattices, knots—are mathematical objects. Drawn in minds, generated by language and computers, these virtual objects rather than the "moderate-sized specimens of dry goods" so favored by analytic philosophy instantiate matter at the extremity of its existence.[8]

Mathematical objects are as lively as lumpy ones, with minds of their own, for since its inception the discipline has debated whether its theorems are discovered or invented.[9] Take the simplest properties of some familiar objects, for example, that every triangle (in the Euclidean plane anyway) has internal angles that add up to 180°, or that the ratio of a circle's circumference to its diameter is always the number pi. The properties obey "forces of mathematical nature" that neither were ever originally anticipated nor can be changed for convenience.[10] If new materialism's "vibrant" matter is "not entirely predictable," neither is mathematical represen-

---

Things (Durham: Duke University Press, 2010). The work of Gilles Deleuze is an important common denominator in much new materialist writing.

[7] Quentin Meillassoux, *After Finitude: An Essay on the Necessity of Contingency*, trans. Ray Brassier (London: Continuum, 2008), 3–4. Meillassoux's work challenges this position.

[8] J.L. Austin, *Sense and Sensibilia*, Reconstructed from the Manuscript Notes by G.J. Warnock (Oxford: Oxford University Press, 1962), 8.

[9] For a review of the long-standing debate within mathematics between nominalism and realism (aka Platonism), see John P. Burgess and Gideon Rosen, *A Subject With No Object: Strategies for Nominalistic Interpretation of Mathematics* (Oxford: Clarendon Press, 1997).

[10] Paul Lockhart, *Measurement* (Cambridge: Belknap Press, 2012), 36.

tation, which keeps surprising by escaping our intentions.[11]

Classically tetradic in composition, matter gets squared away in this essay under four governing categories: *hyle*; extension; transformations; and spoonfuls. Three moments in the geometry of matter measured, mapped, and modeled are plotted: from the classical era as *hyle*, drawing on hylomorphism; from the early modern period as extension in the coordinate plane; and from the modern period as topological transformation. In the fourth quadrant, we circle the square with Trevisa's inventory of measuring utensils to speculate about the future of matter.

HYLE

Hyle is the term Aristotle uses for matter, an everyday word for wood or timber that acquires a secondary, abstract application, much as Plato uses the verb *idein* (to see) and associated vision-related words to coin ideas and theories. The abstractions of Greek philosophy are secondary, originating from the concrete as its primary meaning. As we will see, the Greek concept of matter never loses its intimacy with lumpiness.

Hylomorphism is the term philosophers subsequently ascribed to Aristotle's general argument that all physical things combine two principles: matter and form, the latter designated by various terms including *morphe* (meaning outward appearance, shape) and *eidos*. In one of Aristotle's illustrative examples, a marble statue of Hermes, marble provides the stuff or matter, which, until chipped into the form of Hermes, is aschematic, amorphous, ataxic; that is, unshapely, formless, and wanting in purposeful arrangement.[12] Matter is indeterminate until form imposes shape upon it. The limitations of the example, however, quickly become apparent, for this allegedly shapeless block of marble nonetheless has its own kind of rectilinear or unhewn shape. The point is that the minute *hyle* exists in the specific instance it already exists as an object of some shape, however unplanned or temporary. There will be no specific example of *hyle* that is not already informed, a matter-form composite. *Hyle* is thus less shapeless stuff than it is stuff losing

[11] For the unpredictability of matter, see Bennett, *Vibrant Matter*, 36.
[12] Aristotle, *The Physics*, 190b5–15, trans. Philip H. Wicksteed and Francis M. Cornford, rev. edn. (Cambridge: Harvard University Press, 1957), 76–79.

one shape to gain another. It possesses the capability-of-being-different, the ability to be produced; it is "something to start with;" it "stands under" change as does a "substance," persistent, characterized by potentiality and "not yet," terms perhaps less tainted than that of "privation."[13] Paradoxically, *hyle*—considered in its prime state when free of all specific determinations—turns out to be a concept as metaphysical as *morphe*, never empirically isolatable in a pure state.

Aristotle seems to intend two meanings (at least) by *hyle*'s partner, form. The first meaning is a thing's determinate "shape," sometimes designated by *schema*. In this sense form can be thought of as a boundary line around that which separates one body of matter from another. In the case of two statues being absolutely identical in shape, they would still remain different objects because matter, as Aquinas puts it, is the individuating principle (*principium individuationis*).[14] This sense of form qua shape leads to its second meaning: two statues of Hermes might differ in minor details—height, the size of the nose, and so on; but the shape must be identifiably his, distinctive to his nature. The *schema*, that is, is not randomly imposed from without but arises from within, from what it means to be Hermes. In this teleological turn from boundary to nature, form now refers to a thing's function, to what makes one nature definitionally distinct from another.[15] The shape of a thing should properly be determined by what it naturally is.

Hyle comes to us in closed, determinate shapes made recognizable by their form (*morphe*). Boundary lines emerge from within, teleologically, in the mode of the oak tree taking its characteristic shape from the acorn. *Hyle* fills the space its form requires. And in the terrestrial sphere, where the four elements reign in their discrete jurisdictions, the position *hyle* adopts is determined by its elemental nature. If allowed its druthers, *hyle* will be exactly where it ought to be, occupying a unique place in the cosmos. That tree, which gives the Greeks their very word for matter, is at home in the universe.

The best examples of this relation between shape and nature or definition turn out to be geometric. A closed trilateral

[13] See editorial comments in Aristotle, *Physics*, 69–71.

[14] Thomas Aquinas, *Summa Theologiae*, Vol. 11, 1a 75.4 corp; 1a 75.5 corp, ed. and trans. Thomas Gilby (Oxford: Blackfriars, 1970).

[15] Bertrand Russell, *History of Western Philosophy*, 2nd edn. (London: Routledge, 1991), 177–180.

figure with two of its three sides equal is by definition an isosceles triangle, as Euclid points out in Book I of his *Elements*. Hermes might have legs of unequal length yet still be Hermes, but shorten one of the two equal legs of an isosceles and it becomes a scalene triangle; tilt the angle of the section through a cone and the ellipsis turns into a parabola. The definition of a geometrical figure and its outline are mutually constitutive. That geometric figures should best demonstrate for classical thought the connection between seeming and being says much about how the representation of matter has changed between then and now.

> Of all the differences between Greek and modern mathematics, the most fundamental concerns the role of geometry in each. One might say that the history of nineteenth-century mathematics is the history of the replacement of geometry by algebra and analysis.[16]

Precisely because of this relation between being and seeming, geometric proofs ultimately appeal to demonstration, deixis, self-evidence (note the embedded *videre* in "evident"). The ancient intimacy between seeing and knowing makes intuition the ultimate condition of knowledge, the "I see it!" affirmation.[17] The turn from geometric to algebraic and analytic proof will generate different kinds of measurement. Counter-intuitive and dealing with infinite dimensions beyond any sensory apprehension, modern mathematical proofs now rest heavily on a rigorous logic to navigate beyond the visible.[18] A Venn diagram might confirm set-theoretic relations, but only membership tables can prove them.[19]

The geometric bent helps explain two long-recognized general preferences in classical art for static and closed figures. Euclidean geometry deals with closed line segments rather than lines that stretch endlessly in both directions. "Straight-line motion is never completed. The Greeks preferred circular motion," for the concept of infinity seems

---

[16] Ian Mueller, *Philosophy of Mathematics and Deductive Structure in Euclid's* Elements (Cambridge: M.I.T. Press, 1981), 1.

[17] Mueller, *Philosophy of Mathematics*, 1–10. Ian Stewart, *Concepts of Modern Mathematics*, 3rd edn. (Mineola: Dover Books, 1995), 12.

[18] Stewart, *Concepts of Modern Mathematics*, 1–3.

[19] Stewart, *Concepts of Modern Mathematics*, 54–55.

"formless and confused."[20] That is, infinity sounds much like pure matter—formless and conceptually undefinable. Just as a line cannot be measured until it has been closed off, so *hyle* is unknowable until it has been given determinate being by form. In the hylomorphic paradigm, being real means having a closed and thus measurable shape. In this way Greek materiality stays close to the concrete.

Everything empirically real arises as the result of the labile marriage between two principles, form and matter, that are codependent yet incompatible. If matter individuates form it also resists form and always escapes being defined by it. By distinguishing itself into two principles thus, hylomorphism introduces inevitable discrepancy between a thing's *schema* or *taxis* of itself and its material individuation.[21] Every empirical object is definitionally at odds with itself. No representation in space of a point can satisfy Euclid's definition of it as that which has no part for there is no point we draw that could not be drawn smaller; by the same logic, no drawing of a line can achieve length without breadth and no surface can have length and breadth without width. As a consequence, matter easily becomes typecast as resistance to form. Only in that ideal space of synthetic Euclidean geometry, where matter is intelligible ("noetic") and not sensible ("aesthetic"), are form and matter happily wed.[22]

EXTENSION

Through René Descartes' dualist division between *res cogitans* (mind) and *res extensa* (body), matter gets mechanized. What occupies space (*res extensa*) cannot think and what thinks (*res cogitans*) cannot occupy space and therefore cannot be measured. Consciousness and extension thus become logical opposites:

> Thus extension in length, breadth and depth constitutes the nature of corporeal substance; . . . Everything else

---

[20] Morris Kline, *Mathematics in Western Culture* (rprt. London: Penguin, 1990), 77–78.

[21] For uses of *schema* and *taxis*, see Aristotle, *Physics*, 190b5–30 (76–79).

[22] Aristotle, *Metaphysics*, 1045a34–35, ed. and trans. Hugh Tredennick, 2 vols. (Cambridge: Harvard University Press, 1933-1935), 1:424–425. See also 2:1076a–1093b.

which can be attributed to body presupposes extension, and is merely a mode of an extended thing; ... For example, shape is unintelligible except in an extended thing; and motion is unintelligible except as motion in an extended space. ... By contrast, it is possible to understand extension without shape or movement.[23]

Much as he systematically doubts everything in the *Meditations* in order to arrive at pure *cogito*, so Descartes here conducts a thought experiment in which he strips away all the secondary qualities of a body (color, density, etc.) to reduce it to its first term—sheer extensibility. In contrast to the Aristotelian paradigm where form emerges from within as a consequence of being, the shapes of these extended bodies are epiphenomenal. Indeed, there comes a point in Descartes' consideration of extension when void or empty space cannot be distinguished from *res extensa* considered pure and apart from any body's secondary determining qualities:

> After this examination we will find that nothing remains in the idea of body, except that it is something extended in length, breadth, and depth; and this something is comprised in our idea of space, not only of that which is full of body, but even of what is called void space.[24]

Descartes distinguishes void space (*vacuum*) from a vacuum proper, which, he says, is "repugnant to reason." By void space he means sheer undifferentiated extension in three dimensions, a zone in which nothing sensible is contained

---

[23] Descartes, *The Principles of Philosophy*, part 1 §LIII, in *The Philosophical Writings of Descartes*, Vol. I, trans. John Cottingham, Robert Stoothoff, and Dugald Murdoch (Cambridge: Cambridge University Press, 1985), 210. "Nempe extensio in longum, latum & profundum, substantiae corporeae naturam constituit; ... Nam omne aliud quod corpori tribui potest, extensionem praesupponit, estque tantum modus quidam rei extensae; ... Sic, exempli causa, figura nonnisi in re extensa potest intelligi, nec motus nisi in spatio extenso; ... Sed e contra potest intelligi extensio sine figura vel motu": *Oeuvres de Descartes*, ed. Charles Adam and Paul Tannery, Vol. 8, part 1 (Paris: Librairie philosophique J. Vrin, 1964), 25.

[24] Descartes, *Principles of Philosophy*, part 2 §XI (*Philosophical Writings*, 227–228). "Ita enim advertemus, nihil plane in ejus idea remanere, praeterquam quod sit quid extensum in longum, latum & profundum: quod idem continetur in idea spatii, non modo corporibus pleni, sed ejus etiam quod vacuum appellatur" (*Oeuvres*, 46).

yet which is still inhabited by substance.[25] In this way he rei-
fies space, making of it a thing in itself, infinitely small and
divisible where its axes of extension converge on zero in the
Cartesian plane and endlessly big and multipliable where its
ends expand to infinity.[26] Unlike *hyle*, which is a relational
term, meaningless without *morphe*, *res extensa* achieves
conceptual autonomy qua empty space.

By representing matter as pure extension, Descartes also
represents it as pure measurability, a concept now able to
dispense with all specific instantiations of matter measured.
With no determining qualities that make one particle different from another, matter extends uniformly in all directions.
Measurement itself becomes standardized. Unlike Einstein's
spacetime, Cartesian space does not curve and warp; unlike
natural place in Ptolemaic cosmology, it does not suddenly
get earthy or airy. Descartes concludes that in homogeneous
space, a body set in motion must necessarily continue in
motion at a uniform rate; in this respect also it differs from a
body set in motion in the Ptolemaic system, which speeds up
as it nears its natural elemental home. And a moving body,
lacking any interaction with any other body, necessarily
moves in a straight line.[27] Descartes' laws of nature, published earlier than but more commonly known as Newton's
first law of motion, spell out the uniformity of space, matter
and measurement that characterizes scientific mechanism.

The uniformity of Cartesian matter sunders Aristotle's
organic connection between shape and nature. Form (*morphe*) is imposed from without onto undifferentiated matter
that, lacking consciousness, has no ability to determine how
it ordains itself in space. The shape that *res extensa* acquires
is supervenient, not an identity with its definition. Bodies, of
course, continue to acquire their "natural" shapes—oak trees
grow from acorns and geometric figures still conform their
outline to definition—but a deep formalism now holds apart
material objects (mathematical or concrete) from the system
of rules that makes them meaningful. If hylomorphism introduces an inevitable disconnection between a body's material presence and its form, Cartesian dualism makes official

[25] Descartes, *Principles of Philosophy*, part 2 §XVI–XVIII (*Philosophical Writings*, 229–231).
[26] Descartes, *Principles of Philosophy*, part 2 §§XX–XXI (*Philosophical
Writings*, 231–232).
[27] Descartes, *The Principles of Philosophy*, part 2 §XXXVII and XXXIX
(*Philosophical Writings*, 240–242).

the division between what an object is and anything that can be posited of it, including its measurements. Representation now speaks wholly for mute matter.

The definitive step in this erasure of material reality by conceptual representation comes later in Kant's assertion that space—container of all objects and form of all perceptions—exists in the mind rather than in the empirical world.[28] Tellingly, Kant turns to geometry and arithmetic to make his argument that a priori truth may emerge through synthetic judgments borne of experience (construction and calculation). The mind's intervention is necessary, its representations constituting the only way to experience things that in themselves are unavailable to human cognition. Refusing this refusal to claim access to the thing in itself, new materialism seeks after the incalculable in matter, what is "intrinsically resistant to representation," a materiality characterized now by intensity rather than extension.[29] Sidestepping the obvious question of how the incalculable can be registered, we turn to a different one: how does representation speculate even as it calculates?

MATTER TRANSFORMED

Euclidean space, the space also of Descartes and Kant, where parallel lines never meet, will not support the kind of geometry needed to represent such intensities. For this reason we turn to transformational geometry and the fluid forms it measures. Developed in the nineteenth century by Felix Klein it emerges subsequent to Euclidian and coordinate geometry, yet no linear narrative of progress is being propounded here; rather what is drawn out is possibility already inherent within earlier geometries.

Consider one of the more famous of Euclid's theorems (Book I, proposition 5), which demonstrates that the lower angles of an isosceles triangle are equal. Later known as *pons asinorum*, the bridge from which fell those students whose days in geometry class were numbered, the proof involves extending the legs of the triangle an equal length below its base line, subtending triangles from the extremities of those

[28] Immanuel Kant, *Critique of Pure Reason*, ed. and trans. Paul Guyer and Allen W. Wood (Cambridge: Cambridge University Press, 1998). See first section, "On Space," of *The Transcendental Aesthetic* [A22/B37].
[29] Bennett, *Vibrant Matter*, xv–xvi.

extended lines to the diagonal corners of the base line, and inferring from there the equivalence of the internal base angles of the original isosceles triangle.[30] There is an alternative, shorter proof that Charles Dodgson describes in his dramatized dream vision between Euclid and Minos, a college scholar. It is an armchair proof, ingenious in requiring no additional construction, only superposition, mentally achieved "by taking up the isosceles triangle, turning it over, and then laying it down again *upon itself.*"[31]

There is only one problem with the proof, albeit one so intractable that Dodgson's Euclid says that it reminds him of a story about a man who walked down his own throat. In the virtual environment or ideal space where Euclidean figures live, motionless, how can that triangle be provoked to lift itself up, shake a leg, turn around, and lie face down again in the exact same spot? How can it be above and beneath itself, in two places at the same time? It is easy enough to perform the operation experientially by excising a triangle from any flat surface and replacing it back to front, but empirical confirmation is not demonstrable proof. Transformational geometry, however, provides a mathematically defined way of measuring such an operation.

Transformation geometry enables motion without moving any points and develops out of coordinate geometry, where space is gridded and uniquely numbered (x,y) in the Cartesian plane, once and for all, in all directions. Using the simplest of translation functions, it becomes possible to draw two fully congruent figures, with all dimensions equal save for position. So, for example, $\triangle ABC$ can be replicated 4 units up as $\triangle ABC'$ such that $T{:}(x,y) \rightarrow (x,y+4)$. As the word transformation suggests, a determinate *form* is mapped *across* a space.

It is tempting to regard a proof that flips isosceles trian-

---

[30] Roger Bacon in the thirteenth century names the proposition *fuga miserorum* (the rout of wretches). The term *pons asinorum* originally applied to posers in logic and became applied to Euclid's fifth proposition at some later date. See A.F. West and H.D. Thompson, "On Dulcarnon, Elefuga And Pons Asinorum as Fanciful Names For Geometrical Propositions," *The Princeton University Bulletin* 3.4 (1891): 84–88. For this discussion of Euclid's fifth and transformational geometry, see Stewart, *Concepts of Modern Mathematics*, 12–35 (chapter 2).

[31] Charles L. Dodgson, *Euclid and his Modern Rivals*, Act I, scene ii, §6 (London: Macmillan and Co., 1879), 46–48.

gles like pancakes as "modern," to use Dodgson's term, capable of being conceived only by thinkers who have advanced beyond the geometries of Euclid and Descartes, yet this proof by superposition was attributed to the fourth-century mathematician Pappus of Alexandria by the fifth-century philosopher Proclus.

> Pappus has given a still shorter demonstration that needs no supplementary construction, as follows. Let ABC be isosceles with side AB equal to side AC. Let us think of this triangle as two triangles and reason thus: Since AB is equal to AC and AC is equal to AB, the two sides AB and AC are equal to the two sides AC and AB, and the angle BAC is equal to the angle CAB (for they are the same); therefore all the corresponding parts are equal, BC to CB, the triangle ABC to the triangle ACB, the angle ABC to the angle ACB, and angle ACB to angle ABC.[32]

The reasoning holds except for that initial affirmation, "let us think of this triangle as two triangles." That Pappas could imagine one triangle two in violation of the laws of thought shows that Greek mathematics, like any other body of thought, was messier and less unified than history books will state. More importantly it suggests that an idea—heralded in one century as a breakthrough—can appear in another as speculation, a dodgy shortcut, even a mistake. The fundamental question measurement asks is not "how much?" but "what if?"

T:$(x, y) \rightarrow (x, y+4)$ is a rigid transformation because $\triangle ABC$ and $\triangle ABC'$ are exactly the same shape. Isometries will preserve most geometric properties such as angle measure and ratios of distance. Other kinds of transformation, however, will stretch, contract and deform a figure's outline. A similarity transformation allows difference in scaling so that two circles, say, of different radii remain similar even though the geometric properties of length and area as well as position are now different. Affine transformations abandon angle measure. Keep changing up the geometries to eliminate invariant properties. By combining equivalence classes thus in continuous rather than rigid transformations conventional geometric properties capitulate one by one to topological

[32] Proclus, *A Commentary on the First Book of Euclid's Elements*, trans. Glenn R. Morrow (Princeton: Princeton University Press, 1970), 194–195.

transformations, which measure holes rather than spatial ratios.[33] Rigidity of geometric figure and the gridded Cartesian plane go together. There comes a moment when figures so stretch and deform that identifying them by coordinates no longer achieves any kind of useful measurement.

Along with transformational geometry, Felix Klein invented—or discovered—the Klein bottle, a topological figure that can only be constructed in four-dimensional space and that has no inside or outside.[34] If ever there was a candidate for a figure that could walk down its own throat, it is the Klein bottle. Non-Euclidean transformation geometry enables matter to be morphed. By stepping out of conventional Euclidian geometry into topological space a triangle can morph into a mountain range or moon crater or shapeless blob as objects become each other, leveling hierarchies of substance and anatomy. Euclidean figures such as the revered circle, motionless and ontologically distinct from all other figures, in topology becomes homeomorphic with any other closed figure from triangle to blob. Topological proximity cannot be measured any more in the conventional metric of distance or coordinate units. Geographical space no longer determines nearness in any graph or network representation of "reality."

The graphs and networks that mathematically model concrete matter do not attempt to capture the essence of shapes, to match outline with definition as Euclid did, but instead freely deform them, blatantly, egregiously idealizing and reducing physical bodies. The reduction comes at the cost of the material presence of concrete things—a presence always eclipsed by representation. That fatal slippage between representation and the thing represented appears inescapable. Yet it is in the very blatancy and artifice of such topological deformations that possibility resides. Measuring devices—whether machinic like the telescope and Thomas Young's two-slit projector or algorithmic like calculus—enables matter to surprise us. Mathematical representation constitutes both the limit and opportunity of speculation.

[33] H. Graham Flegg, *From Geometry to Topology* (1974; rprt. Mineola: Dover Publications, 2001), 1–17 (chapters 1–2).

[34] Jeffrey R. Weeks, *The Shape of Space*, 2nd edn. (Boca Raton: CRC Press, 2002), 48–58.

SPOONFULS

Taking holy scripture as his body of examples, Trevisa, in his chapter on the measurements of measuring bodies (*de mensuris corporum mensurabilium*) enumerates differently shaped vessels that apportion dry and wet things:

> *a caudroun* [pot]
> *a basket*
> *a syue* [sieve, strainer]
> *a hucche* [chest, box]
> *a vessel*
> *a spoone*
> *a disch*
> *a tonne* [barrel, cask]
> *a comyn sak or a bagge*
> *a litel euelong cribbe ouÞer a panyer* [oblong basket; hamper]
> *a purse*
> *a bolle* [bowl]
> *a crokke* [kettle]
> *a panne*
> *a bacyn* [basin]
> *a boxe*
> *a cuppe*
> *a boket* [bucket]
> a botel [bottle][35]

These receptacles are not standard measures in the way, say, that an American cup is equivalent to half a pint of liquid or 8 ounces of dry material, but they are suited to the purpose. Hence, the entry for spoon:

> *coclear* 'a spoone' is a litel instrument of Þe mesure of Þe mouth and proporcionate Þerto. And ÞerwiÞ Þe honde serueth Þe mouÞe of dyuers metes."[36]

> [coclear: "a spoon," which is a small instrument adapted to the size of the mouth, and with it the hand feeds the mouth different kinds of food.]

---

[35] Trevisa, *On the Properties of Things*, 1375–1380.
[36] Trevisa, *On the Properties of Things*, 1376.

The fundamental sense of *mesure* is "just enough," the right amount for the shape of the thing. It follows that "just enough" is not a constant but a dependent variable according to situation. "For eueriche body haþ his owne dymensioun and mesure."[37] One obvious meaning of the sentence is that every massy body can be measured, but it also means that every body has its *proper* measure. *Mesure* refers both to the sheer efficient capacity to hold quantity and to be sufficient to the occasion, even to maintain balance and observe restraint.[38] There is an ethical aspect to *mesure*, intimately connected to Aristotle's depiction of virtue as the golden mean between excess and defect and to the representation of justice as proportion.

When—as Descartes, Newton and Kant all maintained—space is uniform in all directions, measurement itself becomes uniform and the *mesure* of determinate objects no longer constitutes an ethical limit but simply registers their vital statistics. Dimension is a reified abstraction anterior to any dimensioned thing just as space itself is a reified abstraction prior to objects that inhabit it. In Trevisa's catalogue, however, dimension is not prior to objects but instantiated as portion-measuring containers. As such apportioning utensils become increasingly standardized, dimension itself gains in autonomy from and authority over the objects that measure dimension.

One step in the direction of uniform dimension is the development of the king's standard, "the authorized exemplar of a unit of measure or weight . . . preserved in the custody of public officers as a permanent evidence of the legally prescribed magnitude of the unit."[39] Although the word only appears in Middle English in the fifteenth century, it is in use in this sense from the thirteenth in both Insular French and Insular Latin. The king's standard was not simply the instantiation of abstract dimension but—like stamped money—a royal guarantee of just measure, and it commanded respect accordingly. William Barker, an ill-tempered baker living in late fifteenth-century York, is cited in the city's civic records for various business-related infractions, which include breaking

---

[37] Trevisa, *On the Properties of Things*, 1372.
[38] Oxford English Dictionary (OED), s.v. *measure* (n.). and Middle English Dictionary (MED), s.v. *mesure* (n.).
[39] Oxford English Dictionary (OED), s.v. *standard* (n. and adj.), II.9. And Middle English Dictionary (MED), s.v. *standard* (n.), 5.a,b,c.

the King's Standard, used to measure grain.[40] Somewhere in between just another measuring instrument and a guarantor of abstract measure, the king's standard generalized dimension and yet was an artifact—tangible, heavy, empirically present to the senses, yet fragile.

This concreteness of measurement is apparent in medieval wills as testators inventory household objects for bequeathal. The inventories often refer to the "pottlepot," a common household measure. A pottle comprises an actual measure of liquid (occasionally dry goods): half a gallon.[41] In 1426, Yorkshireman Petrus del Hay bequeaths to his son Robert "one vessel of silver, called 'potelpott'."[42] Seven years later, Margaret Blakburn (of the famous York family), describes the vessel she bequeaths to her son, Nicholas Blackburn, as "a silver pot, a little less than a potell."[43] To daughter Alice Bolton she leaves "two silver vessels called *pottell pots*."[44] Lest there be any doubt about which ones, Margaret identifies them exactly: "one of which is marked with a shield with 7 bars and a dog and an N and a b, the other is marked under the foot with a sign like this ⋀."[45]

Does "pottelpot" name or describe those two particular vessels? The Latin seems to name them—*ij ollas Argenti vocatas pottellpottez*—yet the term is a general description for any vessel of a standard half-gallon measure. The pottle called *pottelpot* is both a standard measure and an artifact. These late medieval wills are full of references that confuse the use-mention distinction—that is, the name function and

---

[40] *York Civic Records: Volume 4*, ed. Angelo Raine, Yorkshire Archaeological Society 108 (Wakefield: Yorkshire Archaeological Society, 1945), 106.

[41] Oxford English Dictionary (OED), s.v. *pottle* (n.1) 1b. Middle English Dictionary (MED), s.v. *potel* (n.).

[42] "Unam ollam argenti vocatam potelpott" in *Testamenta Eboracensia: A Selection of Wills from the Registry at York II*, ed. James Raine, Publications of the Surtees Society 30 (Durham: Andrews & Co., 1855), 11.

[43] "Unam ollam Argenti aliquantulum minus le potell." See *The Blackburns in York: Testaments of a merchant family in the later Middle Ages*, eds. Ann Rycraft and The Latin Project (York: Centre for Medieval Studies, 2006), 26–27.

[44] "ij ollas Argenti vocatas pottellpottez." *The Blackburns in York*, 26–27.

[45] "Quarum una signatur cum scuto de vij Barres et cane et N et b Altera signatur sub pede cum tali ⋀ signo." *The Blackburns in York*, 26–27.

the description function of objects. Although *pottelpot* denotes generally in that its "essence" is to be a half-gallon measure, the wills turn the word into something like a proper name, for it is this one here, the one with the mark under the foot, and no other that is the only possible referent and does not allow of substitutions, and does not generalize. Vessels, especially cups, frequently become anthropomorphized. Take the will of William Nawton, who in 1453 bequeaths a "cup by name a masour, called from old time 'cosyn' [cousin]."[46] Such routine blurring of the line between show and tell helps explain why Trevisa does not distinguish between the measuring thing and the abstract measure— natural place makes the thing and the space it inhabits one and the same. Descarte's universe is full of empty space, Trevisa's (and Aristotle's) one massive inventory of things. And all objects in that inventory, cups and cousins alike, share one feature in common—*mesure.*

The ethical sense of *mesure* is clear in Trevisa's discussion. A thing is justly proportioned according to what it is and does.[47] When the consideration of sufficient size and shape concerns something as inconsequential as a spoon, the elision of measurement and ethics, of size and function, of shape and nature, of seeming and being seems benign enough. But when the size of a nation or gross domestic product or an individual's physique is under discussion, the ideological assumptions about an object's proper *mesure* show themselves to be more loaded. We should take seriously the idea of form as an ethical limit but try nonetheless to keep it distinct from prescriptions about what is "unnatural." The early modern scientists had good reasons for mechanizing matter and freeing shapes from twaddle about essential natures. Yet the lessons to be taken from these outdated spoonfuls of *hyle*—having a cup for a cousin, ethical limits, sufficiency rather than efficiency as the criterion of measurement—seem central to any current consideration of the ecological and to philosophical efforts to rethink matter. Lest it be thought that measurement, always relative, opens a window of certitude onto the real, call it mis-representation. Let us misrepresent more. Pace Leibniz, *miscalculemus.*

---

[46] *Testamenta Eboracensia*, 58.
[47] Oxford English Dictionary (OED), s.v. *measure* (n.).

RECREATION

Lowell Duckert[1]

> If you seek to create, love springs, fountains, precious stones, the high summits of mountains, the layers of the onion, the leaves of the artichoke, the look of the sea lion, germinal cells, children, all filled to bursting with information like blue supergiants.
>
> Michel Serres, *The Troubadour of Knowledge*

After the blood-smeared Brutus cries for "'peace, freedom, and liberty!'" (3.1.111) in front of the confused masses in William Shakespeare's *Julius Caesar* (1599), Antony takes the "pulpit."[2] He knows how to sway the crowd. Unfurling Caesar's will, he proclaims the citizens Caesar's heirs; better yet, "every several man" is to receive "seventy-five drachmas"

[1] I wish to thank the audiences at the 2012 International Congress on Medieval Studies (Kalamazoo) "Ecologies" roundtable and at the GW MEMSI symposium "Ecologies of the Inhuman" in April 2013 for their creative responses, as well as Jeffrey Jerome Cohen for his feedback.

[2] *The Norton Shakespeare*, eds. Stephen Greenblatt et al., 2nd edn. (New York: W.W. Norton, 2008). All quotations from Shakespeare refer to this edition, by act, scene, and line numbers.

(3.1.232). The crowd is outraged by the assassins' deed. But Antony saves the best stipulation for last. What infuriates the plebeians is something even more desirable than these perks, Caesar's *parks*:

> Moreover, he hath left you all his walks,
> His private arbours and new-planted orchards,
> On this side Tiber; he hath left them you,
> And to your heirs for ever, common pleasures,
> To walk abroad, and recreate yourselves.
> Here was a Caesar! when comes such another?
> (3.2.236–241)

Friends, Romans, countrymen, lend me your garden shears. The word "recreate," it seems, can "lift up Olympus" (3.1.75). Or raise a mob. So what is in a word? "Recreation" and its variants are of Middle English origin via Old French and Latin: *recreare* means "to create anew or again, to restore, refresh, revive." Similarly, "re-creation" comes from *recreatio*, "the action or process of restoring," later to be the English formulation of the prefix *re-* ("again") + *creation* (c. 1400s). English verb forms like "recreate" followed shortly thereafter.[3] Although in common day usage we differentiate the two meanings through pronunciation, Shakespeare collapses both. "To walk abroad, and recreate yourselves" is to re-create "yourselves" abroad simultaneously.

Antony—I should say Shakespeare—knew his Latin. In his eulogy, "recreate" signals: (1) to be refreshed with "common pleasures" like "walk[ing] abroad" through "private arbours and new-planted orchards"; (2) the act of re-creation, to "re-create yourselves" by taking this walk; (3) the playwright's re-creation of Caesar's murder for the Globe Theatre in 1599. Indeed, the play dwells on the art of re-creation: "How many ages hence," Cassius wonders, "Shall this our lofty scene be acted over, / In states unborn and accents yet unknown!" (3.1.112–114). Shakespeare's business is in the public recreation known as theatre-going, an activity that re-creates plays "to your heirs forever" (4). Lastly, and this is Antony's strongest point, Caesar cannot be re-created: "When comes such another?" Recreation (and re-creation), in a word, *creates*. And the desire for it, the play cautions, can destroy. The citizens shout that they will "with brands fire all

---

[3] See the Oxford English Dictionary (OED) entries for *recreation, n.1* and *recreate, v.2* in particular.

the traitors' houses" (3.2.244). Rome will burn. "Domestic fury and fierce civil strife," pledges Antony, "Shall cumber all the parts of Italy" (3.1.266-7). Poets and their "bad verses" will be torn apart (3.3.30). As will infants. Read in this context, recreation does not lead to restoration or replenishment, but to pieces aflame. "Cry 'havoc' and let slip the dogs of war" (3.1.276), "Revenge! About! Seek! Burn! Fire! Kill! Slay!" (3.2.196) shout the plebeians in unison. This is the course of recreation, the "walk" that Antony imagines in his holocaustic vision: "Mischief, thou art afoot. / Take thou what course thou wilt" (3.2.250). Recreation is all the rage—and it still is today. When the United States government shut down from October 1-17 2013, so did the National Park Service. Across the country, civilly disobedient citizens threatened to illegally trespass (and more).[4] *For recreation is a powerful word.*

ARBORS AND ORCHARDS: AN ESSAY ON NON/HUMAN CONDITIONS

In his ample essay, *Gardens: An Essay on the Human Condition*, Robert Pogue Harrison argues that studying the "forces of cultivation" at work in man-made gardens encourages what he calls a "vocation of care."[5] Gardens show "the mark of Cura," "a signature of the human agency to which they owe their existence" (7). No one is better at exemplifying this mark, he believes, than the gardener (25). Care is loosely defined as "an expansive projection of the intrinsic ecstasy of life," while life is "an excess . . . the self-ecstasy of matter. Care in turn is a world-forming, ethically laden extension of . . . terra-forming forces" (33). In a way, Harrison's attention to enchantment (39) and "self-ecstasy" nearly aligns his study with the "vital materialism" of Jane Bennett.[6] Yet as one could surmise by the subtitle of his book, *Gardens* cultivates a humbler kind of anthropocentrism. Gardens "mark our

[4] Utah parks were particularly targeted: http://www.npr.org/blogs/the-two-way/2013/10/09/231086726/county-in-utah-threatens-take over-of-national-park-areas.

[5] Robert Pogue Harrison, *Gardens: An Essay on the Human Condition* (Chicago: University of Chicago Press, 2008), xi.

[6] See Jane Bennett, *Vibrant Matter: A Political Ecology of Things* (Durham: Duke University Press, 2010) and also her book *The Enchantment of Modern Life: Attachments, Crossings, and Ethics* (Princeton: Princeton University Press, 2001).

separation from nature even as they draw us closer to it" (41). In the face of this alienation, the gardener must endlessly toil: it is only through the "gardener's activism—the painstaking, compensatory work of fostering the saving power of human culture" (161), that environmental destruction (by humans) may be curbed. "Without gardeners there would be no future," he baldly claims (37). Thus human agency is *less* distributed amongst arborous things and *more* of a salvific force. Herein lies the paradox, Harrison believes: as we both dread and chase after imaginary paradises, as desire desires more of itself, "our attempts to re-create Eden amount to an assault on creation" (165). Instead, we "need to make ourselves at home on an earth that does not necessarily make room for us" (48) and yet is "a garden we were called on to keep" (176). The human gardener, we might say, helps show us what condition our ecological condition is in. Go ahead: make yourself at home. Just remember: human happiness is something that "only caretaking [fulfills]" (166).

To Harrison's worthwhile attempt to cultivate a better commons—he is right to check the callous hand of human mastery—I wish to think beyond what I believe to be several self-restricting confines of his book: his admission of an unreachable natural order that still implies a sense of order;[7] the nonhuman dependence upon human care; the implied division of nature from culture; his limiting of (a) life to *animate* matter. At these moments we must ask ourselves: can we tell better narratives about co-habitation? Better yet: could Shakespeare? The early modern period has plenty of garden spaces ripe for investigation, as many critics have proven;[8] and yet, I fear that garden studies may just as easily replicate an ethos of human separation and salvation. By decentering the human gardener—by questioning the reality of a "center" itself—this essay attempts to formulate a different recreational ethic. "Garden" comes from the Old English word *geard* for "building, home, region" and is related etymologically to "orchard" through "yard."[9] Thus Caesar's (and

---

[7] Harrison maintains that "we must always remember that nature has its own order and that human gardens *do not* . . . bring order to nature; they give order to our relation with nature" (*Gardens*, 48).

[8] A good example is Rebecca Bushnell, *Green Desire: Imagining Early Modern English Gardens* (Ithaca: Cornell University Press, 2000). Thomas Hill's *The Gardener's Labyrinth* (1577) is a popular primary source.

[9] Simon Schama, *Landscape and Memory* (New York: Vintage Books,

Caesar's) orchard may help us think outside of "park" (which means "pen") and more in terms of the "household," the *eco-* of "ecology." Allow me a quick walk-through: (1) the play highlights the violence of political ambition set against environmental enmeshment, (2) a position that magnifies the historical struggles centered around the creation of London's first park, Moorefields, and that (3) unfortunately extends to the present-day in the outdoor sensation known as "Shakespeare in the Park." I argue that such struggles in the name of recreation may redefine, or "recompose,"[10] the human body, the civic park, and the theatrical playspace as nature-culture hybrid sites, as *more-than* spaces. These truly *creative* sites adumbrate an environmental ethics that would make room for as many beings as possible, one that offers alternatives to reinvigorated georgic modes (human stewardship) as our sole future. While stressing the costs of human agency is necessary, we should also make room for those nonhuman powers that constitute our pullulating world; in short, we must open our recreational ambits to healthy modes of survival, as I will show, and become more intimate. But maybe I am too idealistic, you claim, just as the would-be emperor uttered before his death: "He is a dreamer. Let us leave him. Pass!" (1.2.26). Leave me, ghost of Caesars past! Instead of passing up this opportunity, I will seize it—this is the motto of the conspirators, after all: "There is a tide in the affairs of" non/humans (4.2.270). Make room! Walk with me.

TO WALK ABROAD: ROMAN HOLIDAY?

"Is this a holiday?" Flavius asks the "idle creatures" in the play's second line (1.1.1–2). *Julius Caesar* opens with an interrogation of things walking abroad when they "ought not walk" (1.1.3). In a famous exchange the night before Caesar's death, Casca and Cicero perambulate in an elemental tempest: seas swell as high as the clouds, fire drips from above (1.3). Walking the streets with strangers who unnaturally walk—lions, "men all in fire" (1.3.25)—signal bad times to come for Casca: "they are portentous things / Unto the climate that they point upon" (1.3.28–32). Cicero emphasizes how meaning is *created* out of this chaos: "But men may construe things after their fashion, / Clean from the purpose of

1995), 534.
[10] See Bruno Latour, "An Attempt at a 'Compositionist Manifesto,'" *New Literary History* 41 (2010): 471–490.

the things themselves" (1.3.34–95). Cassius replies with a sense of intentionality: when things change from "their ordinance, — / Their natures, and perform̀ed faculties, / To monstrous quality," he warns, the heavens have made them "instruments of fear and warning / Unto some monstrous state" (1.3.66–71). As above, so below. Both Casca and Cassius depend on a kind of ordered chaos: there *is* meaning (Caesar's dictatorship) behind the madness for the first, while Cicero, master orator and symbol of rhetorical logic, asserts humans' ability to render even the most phantasmic phenomena into rational explanations. Yet the things themselves exert their disruptive force: "this disturb̀ed sky / Is not to walk in" (1.3.39–40). By this conversation, one would not think to recreate oneself in the play: overall, walks are coded dangerous and infectious, acts of vulnerability. Calpurnia bids Caesar not to walk on the Ides: "Think you to walk forth? / You shall not stir out of your house today" (2.2.8–9). Portia recognizes Brutus's sick garden state of mind: "And is it physical / To walk unbrac̀ed and suck up the humours / Of the dank morning?" (2.1.260–262). "You have some sick offence within your mind" (2.1.267), she tells him. The ghost of Caesar walks abroad on the eve of battle. "Caesar, now be still" (5.5.50) are Brutus's last words, suicide his last option to still the restless walkers who torment him. Do not walk, the play appears to caution: there are too many natural (damp) and supernatural (undead) things in the world that ceaselessly stir and move out of their "ordinance."

We will have heard "walk" ten times before we get to Caesar's will; verily, we are set up for "wary walking" (2.1.15) by this point in the play. Antony's promise, then, would seem to falter. But to the unpredictable "walk" and "walks abroad" that threaten others, Caesar and his favorite take control in a ecopolitical way: via the "ambit" of "ambition." "Ambit" comes from the Latin *ambitus* ("circuit") from *ambire* ("go around") and thus could mean "precincts, environs" and the canvasing of votes that "ambition" connotes. Though not related etymologically, their *ambulations* have highly-restricted ambits. In regards to the pernicious outside world, they do not make room for it, preferring to keep stray things at a distance or contain them within inside/outside circuits. The conspirators recognize this policy: Caesar's body, Cassius believes, is out of bounds, encompassing everything, a "Colossus"; they "walk under his huge legs and peep about / To find ourselves dishonourable graves" (1.2.142, 136–139). The co-assassinators are literally "*under*lings" (1.2.142, my emphasis). For his attempts to enclose Rome itself (thereby making it a garden dictator state), Caesar deserves to die: "When could they say till now, that talk'd of Rome, / That her wide walls encompass'd but one man? / Now it is Rome indeed and room enough, / When there is in it but only one man" (1.2.155–158). By Cassius's definition, Rome feels the squeeze of a near-imperial ambit that they feel obligated to curtail. And we all know what Brutus thought about Caesar: he persuades the plebeians to think that "he was / ambitious" (3.1.25) before Antony takes his turn. His follow-up famously repeats "ambitious" seven times during his speech; the point cannot be missed: "he [Caesar] was ambitious" (3.2.83). But why should the mob care? Antony in fact turns ambition to his advantage by playing upon the plebeians' love of circuitous spaces that they wish to go around. Caesar *was* ambitious by forcing the landscape into a particular ambit—an enclosed garden space—for which they should be thankful. This Colossus labored every day for their holidays. Antony says to walk *this* way, and they follow.

Lost in this debate concerning Roman "walks" and censured over-steppers, however, is any room for the nonhuman; there is not "room enough" for "new planted orchards." In this anthropocentric political arena, any democracy of objects accedes to an empire of subjects.[11] Shakespeare accentuates the persistency of this *central* strategy, for it carries on after Caesar's death, re-arriving like a ghost in the figure of Antony. When Antony descends from the pulpit, he makes a "ring" around him (3.2.158); his new ambit puts him at the center of relations, and from the "hearse" bearing Caesar's body, no less: "Over thy wounds now do I prophesy" (3.2.159; 3.1.262). This soon-to-be-triumvir extends the Roman will of ambition to environ the disruptive environment. Anything out of order is met with aggression; when the "sweaty" populace with "stinking breath" comes too close (1.2.244–245), Anthony exclaims: "Nay, press not so upon me. Stand farre off" (3.2.161). All the plebeians obey: "Stand back! Room! Bear back!" (3.2.162). Even when the nonhuman gains expression, it is to echo a human voice for justice: "a tongue / In every wound of Caesar that should move / The stones of Rome to rise and mutiny" (3.2.219–221). One deals with wayward things that "walk abroad" by hacking them back, denying them their voice—by *pruning,*

[11] I borrow this phrase from Levi Bryant, *The Democracy of Objects* (Ann Arbor: Open Humanities Press/MPublishing, 2011).

in a word. "[T]his foul deed shall smell above the earth," Antony believes, but he is wrong (3.1.277). *Caesar* not only exposes the anthropocentricity of recreation, it also shows its potential damages: just as Rome must be sawed through civil war in order to re-create itself, the Tiber must be tamed and hewn for its citizens to recreate themselves. Staring at the corpse of Caesar, Antony conflates both acts of violence in a short phrase: "O pardon me," he cries, "thou bleeding piece of earth" (3.1.257). And in the name of Roman re-creation, the "earth" *will* bleed. Shakespeare magnifies the third position through Antony's lament. So I repeat Flavius's question: "Is this a holiday?" *This?* A too-human form of recreation overlooks the stuff *by* which we are encompassed, *with* which we "go around," and *of* which we are made: "thou . . . earth." Is it first war, then peaceful holiday, Antony? No: first war, then war. *For recreation is a powerful word.*

THIS SIDE TIBER, THIS SIDE THAMES

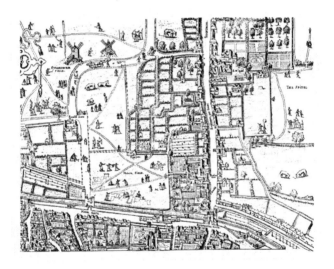

Figure 1: Map of London drawn by Anthonis van den Wyngerrade (1558) and engraved by Franciscus Hogenberg (1559). Moorgate and Moorfields are center-left. Note the strollers and washers within the park, and a lone figure (peeing?) on the left.

I have been arguing that *Caesar*'s parks matter, and suffer, through human ambitions. I now wish to illustrate how this recreational struggle in the play revealed—indeed intensi-fied—early modern English green desires as well as disputes. As D.J. Hopkins argues, *Caesar* is a "*performance archive*" that manifests "the history of one of the major urban devel-opments in London during this period: the emergence of the public theatre," thereby demonstrating the co-production of urban space.[12] "More than just a site in representation, early modern London was equally produced in performance" (48). As a Roman city once known as "Londinium" (founded c. 50 C.E.), its streets and stages displayed hybridizations of past and present, like James I's triumphal entry in 1604 (46–47). Since Hopkins is engaged primarily with conceptions of civic space, I wish to extend his argument about performative hybridity to nature-culture spaces in early modern England as well. I believe that the play was partly in response to, and led to a movement for, "common pleasures" in London. There are reasons why the play's "private arbours and new-planted orchards" were points of contention for audience members: Caesar's will discloses the lack (actually, nonexist-ence) of civic parks for London's own plebeians. Historian Keith Thomas notes that while public parks were not popular until after the Restoration, "in the early modern period planting for ornament and amenity gained momentum, par-ticularly in the towns."[13] Trees in Londoners' gardens were common since the twelfth century. Flowers appealed to townsfolk and most Tudor homes had gardens of some sort where they could grow food. Norwich was once known as a budding "garden city," described as "'either a city in an or-chard or an orchard in a city, so equally are houses and trees planted'" (205). Orchards like these could confuse distinc-tions between "natural" and "built" environments, city and country, and commoners increasingly found in these hybrid middles aesthetic rather than mere use value: "Trees . . . were now planted and cherished for amenity's sake alone" (204).

Yet the desire for pleasure planting had its aggressive side. In this brief ecomaterial history I am trying to trace, we

---

[12] D.J. Hopkins, "Performance and Urban Space in Shakespeare's Rome, or 'S.P.Q.L.,'" in *Rematerializing Shakespeare: Authority and Representation on the Early Modern English Stage*, eds. Bryan Reyn-olds and William N. West (New York: Palgrave Macmillan, 2005), 40.

[13] Keith Thomas, *Man and the Natural World: Changing Attitudes in England 1500-1800* (New York: Oxford University Press, 1983), 204. The following historical information comes from Chapter 5 ("Trees and Flowers"), section ii ("Tree-Planting").

can glimpse several possible reasons why English plebeians would rampage along the Thames for their greener spaces. Aristocratic planting was a large-scale operation: Elizabethans like Sir William Hatton were commended for planting groves (206), and such practices helped solidify class lines. Later domestic gardening would become less of an extension of nature-culture continuums and more of a magnification of the human logic of improvement ("cultivation").[14] Most controversial, perhaps, was the fact that environmental degradation often involved the displacement of lower social classes. As Thomas famously states:

> Disparking, enclosure of chases, encroachment on the commons, the lax administration of the royal forests and the steady reduction in their extent: all meant the clearing of woodland and the felling of trees. It was not on Tower Hill that the axe made its most important contribution to English history. (193)

Thus the recreational desire for parks sprung from such crises as the deforestation of local and national forests at the turn of the seventeenth century, the rapidly diminishing amount of ready wood as a consequence, and the increasing "'de-ruralization' of the towns." I will not go into too much detail here concerning historical enclosure regulations or royal and aristocratic hunting privileges in relation to Shakespeare's plays—this has been done intelligently elsewhere.[15] But I do want to speculate on what "private arbours" would have conjured in his audiences' minds. Probably "parks," royal forests protected by law; in Thomas's opinion, royal conservation still stands as a notable attempt to conserve a large part of England, its game, and the growing interests in deer parks. Even so, it is not too far-fetched to think that An-

[14] The Duke of Beaufort, for example, placed his house in the center of a star cut from the forest, demonstrating, in Thomas's estimation, "his power to manipulate the lives and environment of lesser mortals and emphasized the all local avenues of power converged upon him" (207).

[15] See, for example, Todd A. Borlik, *Ecocriticism and Early Modern English Literature: Green Pastures* (New York: Routledge, 2011), esp. Chapters 2 and 5; Vin Nardizzi, *Wooden Os: Shakespeare's Theatres and England's Trees* (Toronto: University of Toronto Press, 2013); and Robert N. Watson, *Back to Nature: The Green and the Real in the Late Renaissance* (Philadelphia: University of Pennsylvania Press, 2006), esp. Chapter 3.

tony's mention could aggravate contemporary class struggles: "the domestic economy of the poor" clashed with the
"recreation of a privileged few" who sought this game (200).
Might Londoners have expressed their dissatisfaction with a
different kind of "green imperialism"?[16] The seizure of Elizabethan royal forest and deer parks did not always precipitate
a transfer to the people—which is what Caesar's imperialism
(the will) had promised to do. Although spaces were susceptible to "disparking" (193) and given to cattle, it is not clear
that the land would have been used specifically for economic
gain; as previously mentioned, planting for aesthetic pleasure was fashionable. Nevertheless, cases of turning arable
land into pleasure gardens for the sake of ornamentation
sometimes involved the dislocation of villages and their in-
habitants. What is clear in all of these conjectures, however,
is that any conflict of the commons, with any amount of
competing desires, must break from the narrow restrictions
of *human* class. Richard Wilson argues in cultural materialist
fashion that *Caesar* leaves "the scars of a material struggle,"[17]
and, likewise, Hopkins's predominantly cultural reading is in
a collection called *Rematerializing Shakespeare*. Yet as we
have seen so far, the early modern English—playgoers and
axemen—were leaving "scars" upon the "material" earth
itself. It is time to rematerialize differently—ecomaterial-
ize—not to repeat issues of class only,[18] but to circumvent
nature/culture and environmental health/justice binaries at
once. Into these variously verdant responses—socio-eco-
nomic, political, and aesthetic—the wooden matter of trees
take the early modern stage.

As a play known for its multitemporality—Rome's anach-
ronistic clocks (2.1), for example—it should not be surprising
that *Caesar* enfolds humans and nonhumans in addition to
past and present. In his innovative book *Wooden Os*, Vin
Nardizzi argues that early modern plays documented the
ecocrisis of wood shortage—multiply defined as forest, gardens, parks, and timber—not only in theatrical representation, but through the exact substance of which props and
theatres were made. Once actors enchanted the "dead

[16] Referring to Richard Grove, *Green Imperialism: Colonial Expan-
sion, Tropical Island Edens and the Origins of Environmentalism
1600-1860* (Cambridge: Cambridge University Press, 1995).
[17] Richard Wilson, *Julius Caesar* (London: Penguin, 1992), 40.
[18] See Nardizzi's *Wooden Os* (59–83) for a smart reading of class and
environmental protest in the staging of *The Merry Wives of Windsor*.

wood" (23) of the playhouse, its materiality challenged inside/outside binaries; audience members, he argues, were already inside the woods: "representations of living trees overlay the playhouse's exterior timbers, reminding viewers that theatres were (made from) trees . . . the theatres disappear behind and into the woods" (27). Props could point up these "darker shades of green" (28), but so could dramatic language. When characters refer to trees in deictic and gestic ways—"yon pine does stand" (4.13.1) from *Antony and Cleopatra*, which might have meant the wooden column of the theatre—they secure the material link between wood and stage, what Nardizzi calls an "evergreen fantasy of the first order . . . cultural reafforestation" (24). Caesar's orchards, then, could tap into this fantasy of "systematic replanting" (12) that was in response to the "rich array of eco-fantasies and nightmares about the shortage of wood and timber" (24). We should also keep in mind that *Caesar* was probably the first play staged at the newly opened wooden O, the Globe, in 1599—a point of material significance. The "this" of Antony's "this side Tiber" then, could draw attention to the disappearing trees along "this side" Thames, out- and inside the Globe, a theatre that marked a noticeable alteration to the Bankside landscape and that, according to contemporary drawings, still had (vulnerable) forest around it. Thus Shakespeare's reference to anything "new-planted" is not just a slavish following of his source, Plutarch.[19] The "darker" greenspace of dramatic production parallels the nightmare landscape that Antony imagines the mob enacting and the play-actor Antony indicates in greater "Londinium" at large and along river: the razed counterpoint to the evergreen fantasy of pleasures for all.

Antony's crowd-piquing tribute to Caesar in 3.2 is more than just a historical wink to the audience or a realization (perhaps foretelling) of their worst ecological nightmares. Less than a decade after the play was first performed, early

[19] From Plutarch's *Life of Marcus Brutus*: "For first of all, when Caesars testament was openly red amonge them, whereby it appeared that he bequeathed unto every Citizen of Rome, 75. Drachmas a man, and that he left his gardens and arbors unto the people, which he had on this side of the river of Tyber, in the place where now the temple of Fortune is built: the people then loved him, and were marvelous sory for him." Quoted in the Arden Shakespeare 3rd edition of *Julius Caesar*, ed. David Daniell (Walton-on-Thames: Thomas Nelson, 1998), 344.

modern English citizens visited London's first civic park. Richard Johnson's *The pleasant walkes of Moore-fields* (1607) divulges Londoners' fervent and verdant desires for recreation, attempting to "set downe a fewe notes of ancient recordes" concerning a ten-acre plot of land called Moorfields near the Moorgate.[20] Opened during the reign of James I, Moorfields outlasted the Great Fire, surviving until a carpeting factory was built there in the mid-eighteenth century. Johnson provides a history of the park and descriptions of several key architectural sites around it, ending with an encomium to London. His opening language creates an interplay between the "ancient" records and the modern city, just like how the "ancient" times of Caesar's classical Rome and the "present-day" early modern city intersect onstage. Adding to this temporal breakdown, he writes his history as an interpolative dialogue between a "London Citizen" and a "Countrey Gentleman," in their exchange attempting an *inter*change between city and country. Taking his readers on a walking tour of pleasures, Johnson is as educational as he is obsequious. The knights and aldermen of London are the great improvers: "Those sweet and delightful walks of More fields (right Worshipfull) as it seemes a Garden to this Citty and a pleasurable place of sweet ayres for Cittizens to walke in," he lauds, "now made most beautiful by your good worships appointment." Both fields and magisterial munificence are on display. "O you flattere[r]!" (5.1) —Antony knows this tactic the best.

Moorfields appears to be the ideal civic pleasure garden: for the people, by the people. Even "Sir *Leonard Holly-day* [Holiday?] then Lord Maior" plants the first tree. Once belonging to two daughters, the land had passed from private to public hands—just what the disgruntled plebeians demand in the play. But speaking more urgently to the historical debates about parks that inform *Caesar*, Moorfields actually arose from civil discontent. Johnson is careful to define the creation of the park as an act of duty; his two-man mob is not that rebellious, but the Citizen tells a story of others who were. Before the reign of Henry VIII, London residents "had so enclosed these fields, with hedges and ditches, that neyther the young men of this City might shoote, nor the ancient persons walke for pleasure in these fields." Some

---

[20] Richard Johnson, *The pleasant vvalkes of Moore-fields Being the guift of two sisters, now beautified, to the continuing fame of this worthy citty* (London: Henry Gosson, 1607).

citizens were "arested for walking, saying, that no Londoner
ought to go out of the Citie, but in the hye wayes." Here is an
early modern day Flavius stopping citizens along the path,
inquiring about their professions, interrupting their holidays.
Walking is regulated. Is this an arbor day? Far from it: the
citizens eventually take matters into their own hands six
years into Henry VIII's reign, when

> a great number of the Citie, assembled themselues in a
> morning and a Turner in a Fooles coat, ran crying the
> rough the Citie, Shouels and spades, Shouels & spades,
> by which meanes followed so many people, that it was a
> wonder to behold, and within lesse than thrée houres all
> the hedges about the Citie were cast downe, the ditches
> filled vp, and euery thing made plaine, such was the
> quicknesse of these diligent workemen, after this the fields
> were neuer more hedged in.

Do not fence us in! the angry mob shouts. But the cry of
"Shouels & spades" is not exactly an anthem of green peace,
either; this is not quite the "fire!" of Antony's mob but it is a
powerful example of citizens seizing their recreational rights
nevertheless, ushering in an environmental policy of conservation (they need to use the land) rather than preservation,
fulfilling a class-specific need: "for Cittizens to walke in to
take the ayre, and for Merchants maides to dry clothes in,
which want necessary gardens at their dwellings." Not everyone owns a garden, it seems, but the Citizen proudly relates this story of civic duty—recreational power to the people—and receives the appropriate awed response from his
country interlocutor. "The Citizens," the Gentleman concurs,
"euer carried gallant minds" and do so "to this day (I sée)."

But just as the play dramatizes the ecological impacts of
civil war on the unwilling third participant "earth," there is
more than a human struggle afoot "to this day." After Moorfields was bequeathed by the "two mayds," but before it became a park, it was "a wast and vnprofitable ground a long
time." Like "this side Tiber," *this* side Thames must be domesticated. To reassure him that he is on firm ground, the
Citizen boasts about their technological feats of drainage:[21]
"Those be the worthy Aldermen and Common-counsell of

---

[21] For more on drainage's dramatic connections, see Todd A. Borlik,
"Caliban and the Fen Demons of Lincolnshire: the Englishness of
Shakespeare's *Tempest*," *Shakespeare* 9.1 (2013): 21–51.

London, who seeing the disorder vsed in these fieldes, haue bestowed this cost, and as occasion requires intends further to beautifie the same." This "disturbèd" sty's disorder is met with the ambits of the honorable park planners. The intention is not as manipulative as Antony's, but the execution is still scarring; it requires a colonization of the moors and fields: This "making" of the beautiful was literally draining. Work had begun in the reign of Henry V,

> whereby these fields were made something more commodious, but not so pleasant and drye as now they are, for many times they stood still full of noisome waters, which afterward in the yeare 1527. was by the meanes of sir *Thomas Semor,* Mayor made dry, who repairing the sluces, conuayed the sayd waters ouer this Towne Ditch, into the course of *Wall-brooke*shoare, and so into the Thames, and by these degrées was this Fen or Moore at length made maine and hard ground.

Not only are the pleasures unprecedented, but so are the park and the amount of leveling labor required to build it, "a thing that neuer hath béen séene before to goe so néere London." Yet what the gentleman cannot "sée" fully is the fens' capacity for "bewildering order"—elemental philosopher David Macauley's phrase for "a kind of chaotic cosmos."[22] Disorder subtends order; the fens keep fighting back and must be necessarily tamed "by these degrées." Beautification proves to be a dirty, unpredictable, and full-time job. Soon after this lesson in landscape architecture, the Gentlemen asks where the water comes from; once the city was divided "by a faire brooke of swéete Water," but

> at length the same by a common consent of this Citty, was arched ouer with Brick, and paued with stone equall with the ground whence it passed thorough: and is now in most places builded vpon, that no man may deserue it, and therefore the trace thereof is hardly known to the common sort of people.

---

[22] David Macauley, *Elemental Philosophy: Earth, Air, Fire, and Water as Environmental Ideas* (Albany: State University of New York Press, 2010), 355. "Our living and evolving world in all its complex and confusing order thus cannot be contained or fully explained by any one account, whatever its pretense to comprehensiveness or objectivity" (355).

These sewers must be cleaned out yearly we are told, for they always spew forth like Caesar's gaping wounds—"Which like a fountain with an hundred spouts / Did run pure blood" (2.2.77–78)—but not so anthropomorphic. The sewers of "Londinium" will "rise and mutiny" again and again (3.2.221). Thus the "antiquities" are never antique. They keep coming into the present to tell histories of environmental alteration.

And arguably, *degradation*: attempting to bury brooks without a trace shows how a specific kind of recreation disavows its own violence through domestication—according to Macauley, "a process that captures, interiorizes, and changes formerly unbridled fluids"[23] —a task applicable to "this side" of any river. Yet these "traces" of silenced riparian things can never disappear. As the Citizen looks upon each object of their tour, what he cannot "sée," but what he still feels, are the nonhuman voices that continue to speak to them. Though the Citizen feels emotion with these beings, he is careful to distinguish inside/outside boundaries. When the Gentleman asks about the stocks, for example, he is told that they are there "as a punishment for those that lay any filthy thing within these fields, or make water in the same to the annoyance of those that walke therein, which euill sauors in times past haue much corrupted mans sences, and supposed to be a great nourisher of diseases." The Citizen's reaction signifies a discomfort with the impure rather than a sympathy for it, or perhaps a recognition that *nothing* is pure. In order to uphold this fantasy of the incorruptible, the fields must be exclusive; vagabonds are not allowed.[24] The same in- and exclusivity applies to the Bridewell Prison nearby. The Citizen's reverie is so disturbed by the vices within, he asks to change the subject. The new topic could not be any *less* soothing: "That place I thinke néedlesse sir to speake of in these walkes, therefore I pray you shew the of the antiquitie of this Monasterie of Bedlem where these two charitable sisters were buried." If vice cannot even be muttered within the park's walls, here we are reminded of the prison for the mentally insane that walls in the park's undesirables. The Citizen

[23] Macauley, *Elemental Philosophy*, 257. See also Chapter 7 ("Domestication of the Elements"), esp. sections "Plumbing Philosophy" and "Watercraft and Landscape Aesthetics."

[24] Consider Feste's doleful song at the end of *Twelfth Night*: "But when I cam to man's estate, / With hey, ho, the wind and the rain, / 'Gainst knaves and thieves men shut their gate" (5.1.380–382).

sees the park as a space invaded by those creatures who "walk abroad" where they are not supposed to. The common, in short, is not so common; its pleasures must be policed in order to be so. Or slowly forgotten. At one point the Gentleman asks what certain stones signify, and he is told that the spring is called *Annis Cla . . . e,* who matching her selfe with a riotous Courtier in the time of *Edward* the first, who vainely consumed all her wealth, and leauing her in much pouertie, there drowned she herself, being then but a shallow ditch or running water." The insane, the pissers, the desolate, and the destitute are at the gate—and they always get in. But such aberrations do not belong here. In order to preserve this boundary of inside/outside, common/wealth, they must either be covered up, drowned, or have the (Moor)gate shut upon them. Their fate is only made worse by the fact that Johnson presents his conversation in the guise of a crossing: a country-city "discourse" that would seem to personify the hybridity of nature-culture. Poor parks and recreation? No: enemies of pleasure at the gate are turned away: here is the true "tragedy of the commons."[25] *For recreation is a powerful world.*

TO YOUR HEIRS FOR EVER . . . EXCEPT COYOTES

Figure 2: A coyote in (?) Griffith Park, Los Angeles.

[25] Garrett Hardin's (infamous) term concerning population growth and resource management in his article "The Tragedy of the Commons," *Science* 162.3859 (1968): 1243–1248.

Up to this point I have discussed the dramatic and civic history of London recreation and the stakes of constraining the ambits of things walking abroad. *Caesar* asks us to pay attention to the fine line between alteration and degradation, how the commons are constructed and who its members are. Though we have inherited Wilson's practice we do not have to perpetuate it. Though we are Caesar's (and *Caesar*'s) heirs, we may check our impulses to "recreate [our]selves" and pursue different recreational roles in future. I now wish to talk about recreation as a combination of performance (a play) and civic history (a park) through a popular recreation at the moment: outdoor festivals often heralded as "Shakespeare in the Park." Lawrence Buell has recently prophesized that environmental criticism is a "project in motion."²⁶ More to my interests here, drama gives this project a unique momentum: "Dramatic performance always requires and reproduces physical environments . . . . But in performance, environmentality is underscored and its residual potentialities multiplied" (48). Ecocriticism's progenitors knew this. In *The Comedy of Survival: Literary Ecology and a Play Ethic* (1974), arguably the first work of environmental criticism, Joseph Meeker opposes the anthropocentric and environmentally-destructive genre of tragedy to what he calls the "comic way . . . the path of reconciliation."²⁷ This way "connects us with other species through shared evolutionary history, and through present play that crosses species lines. Comedy is a contributor to survival, and a habit that promotes health" (11).

With *Hamlet* as *Survival*'s centerpiece, Meeker's study, coincidently, is also early modern. But how can Shakespearean festivals in the rough help us navigate the "way . . . the path"—or to use *Caesar*'s term, "walks"—today? Take the example of *Hamlet* in Los Angeles's Griffith Park. When the local Independent Shakespeare Company (ISC) staged the play in September of 2011, audiences were annoyed by the howls of coyotes. "Angels and ministers of grace defend us!" indeed (1.4.20). Once, during their free summer festival, a company member grew frustrated when soliciting donations: "Can someone shoot that coyote?"²⁸ This exclamation

²⁶ Lawrence Buell, *The Future of Environmental Criticism: Environmental Crisis and Literary Imagination* (Malden: Blackwell, 2005), ix.
²⁷ Joseph Meeker, *The Comedy of Survival: Literary Ecology and a Play Ethic*, 3rd edn. (Tucson: University of Arizona Press, 1997), 14.
²⁸ Ian Lovett, "Baying at the Bard, Appropriate or Otherwise," in *The*

is really a request to purify the playspace of its nonhuman actors. Boundaries between the "outside" (nature) and "inside" (high culture) are insurmountable, it seems, and not just because the company's stage sits in the natural amphitheater of the Old Zoo. *Hamlet*'s coyotes force us to see how emplacement has become an increasingly important topic to consider in our world where species *howl* and where the complex relationships between humans and nonhumans can just as easily be met with a gun rather than "reconciliation." Seven Griffith Park coyotes, in fact, were tracked and killed in 2009 after two biting incidents were reported (one involved nibbling a sleeping man's toe). A public outcry ensued.[29] The recreation known as "Shakespeare in the Park" brings environmentality center stage: be it a performance in- or outdoors, a territorialized park or "coyote territory."[30] Note how easily the comedy of survival is over: "Can someone shoot that coyote?"

Baying is not playing at the ISC, apparently; and by frightening off would-be patrons, neither is it paying. The request to shoot is similar to the Citizen's desire to shut. Though hundreds of years apart, Moorfields and Griffith Parks beg the question: why are some creatures let into the commons and others are not? Gloucester's rebuke of Regan in *King Lear* says as much: "If wolves had at thy gate howled that dern time, / Thou shouldst have said 'Good porter, turn the key.' / All cruels else subscribed" (3.7.64–66). Some (wolves) are met with compassion and others (coyotes, kings) with segregation. To be sure, Gloucester is responding to what he perceives as the fallen state of nature after Lear's banishment, and possibly privileges the shut-out human because the lupine is *not* usually let indoors (hence the power of his invective: how can a daughter consider that wolves and "all cruels else" are better than her father's reentry?). But he marks the *choice* nevertheless that we all have to open or close ourselves to recreational coexistence. Timothy Morton says as much: "The trouble with love is that it has a tinge of 'evil' about it. Out of the universe of things . . . I select you."[31]

New York Times, September 13, 2011: http://www.nytimes.com/2011/09/14/us/out-here-coyotes-provide-soundtrack-to-theater-in-griffith-park.html.

[29] Karin Klein, "The Coyotes of Griffith Park" in *Los Angeles Times*, September 22, 2009.

[30] Lovett, "Baying at the Bard."

[31] Timothy Morton, *The Ecological Thought* (Cambridge: Harvard

The ISC "turn[s] the key" of closure in Griffith Park, believing, detrimentally to coyotes, in its nature/culture boundedness. Interestingly, the company just finished *As You Like It* in their 2013 season; caught in a lovers' cacophony at the end of the play, Rosalind begs, "Pray you, no more of this; 'tis like the howling of Irish / wolves against the moon" (5.3.101–102). How would audience members react to this derogatory line amidst the coyotes' baying? Or Lear's "Howl, howl, howl, howl!" in that play's denouement (5.3.256)? Rosalind could be speaking to human and nonhuman Angelenos in attendance, a doubly derogatory line directed against an ethnicity as well as a species at once.

The walk from Johnson to the ISC through the common recreational denominator of Shakespeare helps us rephrase Gloucester's tirade as a recreational thought experiment: how *are* we to address the non/human howls at our gates, from "this side Tiber," to the mad of "morish ground," to coyotes? The Friends of Griffith Park outline better alternatives in their Wildlife Management Plan, such as biodiversity surveys and environmental education for park goers.[32] And let us open up further; hearing the language of things that does not merely disrupt our performances but *are* performances proves that we are always performing with a greater cast of characters. I am reminded of Aldo Leopold's landmark essay "Thinking Like a Mountain" for that very reason: he attempts to decipher the "hidden meaning" of the wolf's howl-language.[33] To our attempts to decipher, however, I would add an attempt to *listen* while not necessarily translating these codes into stable meanings. And a yearning to do so, even if we know that this language will always be fuzzy. When Michel Serres hears "The Great Howling of Wolves" in *Biogea*, the howling is not just flora and fauna but *everything*. The gates of the world crash open: "We heard the world open, express itself, clamor, rumble, call, demand, invade, fear, be moved, forbid. I'm telling the story of the world beginning to tell it's [sic] story."[34] These are emotions that

University Press, 2010), 96.

[32] Visit Friends of Griffith Park here: http://www.friendsofgriffith park.org/.

[33] "Those unable to decipher the hidden-meaning know nevertheless that it is there, for it is felt in all wolf country, and distinguishes that country from all other land": Aldo Leopold, *A Sand County Almanac: And Sketches Here and There* (Oxford: Oxford University Press, 1949).

[34] Michel Serres, *Biogea*, trans. Randolph Burks (Minneapolis: Uni-

stress motion, emotions that arrive from the motions of others, like vibrational sound waves: "Everything stirs, of course, everything evolves, everything changes and moves, but by trembling, with emotion . . . Everything speaks. How is it we don't yet have anything said or written in this universal language?" (199). We do: hail, *Caesar*. But is it enough? The transmission importantly requires a response, an ethical signal sent back. Why not make this our recreation? The common—by now which I mean to be non/human things— asks us to listen to its pleas. Never cry coyote? *Do*. A redefined "recreation" can lead to variegations of emotion— "common pleasures" that broadcast as broadly as possible. *For recreation is a powerful word.*

RECREATE YOURSELVES

To conclude, I want to meditate on the creatures of recreation and their lives at stake, the creations to come.[35] Antony's recreation of war compels me to create my own thought experiment. Todd Borlik has advocated for re-thinking dominion from the early modern, state-centered Republic of Nature.[36] And Brutus in the play, of course, proves that "public reasons" (as in, the Roman Republic) are worth fighting for. Some have argued for "compulsory recreation."[37] I recommend that we rethink the "public." What if we reconceived recreation as a doing—an action and a process, yes— but also as an environmental practice that creates creative coexistence, that makes happen, that brings human and nonhuman relationships into being, into "common pleas-

vocal, 2012), 116.

[35] I use the term "creature" deliberately. See Julia Reinhard Lupton, "Creature Caliban," *Shakespeare Quarterly* 51.1 (2000): 1–23.

[36] If Shakespeare was in the middle of these historical debates over the privatization of land (enclosure) when he composed *As You Like It* (1598-1600), he certainly was still thinking of them when he wrote *Julius Caesar* (1599). See "Rethinking Dominion" in Borlik, *Green Pastures*, 181–188.

[37] Deploring the political involvement (or lack thereof) in creating park systems, John Muir wrote that "our crude civilization engenders a multitude of wants, and law-givers are ever at their wits' end devising. The hall and the theater and the church have been invented, and compulsory education. Why not add compulsory recreation?" *John of the Mountains: The Unpublished Journals of John Muir*, ed. Linnie Marsh Wolfe (Madison: University of Wisconsin Press, 1979), 234.

ures," into the Common (the *oikos*)? A "making things public"?[38] The recreational ethics I am proposing asks what ecologies we create, and re-create, and with whom. Who is restored, refreshed, revived, and who is excluded from creation? Recreation is not an activity the autonomous human undertakes, or an enclosed place the human walks through, like an orchard. I suggest that we become more intimate with these beings, for we are always creating with them. There you are, "thou earth." So here is my holiday: when the call to recreate is not a call to arms, but a chance to recreate our shared selves, a call to create, and to love, again, and again, anew. *For recreation is a powerful word.*

---

[38] On "the search for the Common," see Latour, "Attempt at a 'Compositionist Manifesto'" (488). For the "public," see Bruno Latour and Peter Weibel, eds., *Making Things Public: Atmospheres of Democracy* (Cambridge: M.I.T. Press, 2005).

TREES

Alfred Kentigern Siewers

The millennia-old Llangernyw Yew tree in St. Digain's church-yard in North Wales survives in enormous offshoots, having endured an oil tank placed in its middle for a time in the late twentieth century, and the loss of its core. Trees in general likewise endure despite having suffered theoretically at the hands of postmodernism, given Deleuze and Guattari's cri-tique of arboreality as hierarchical, which promoted the rise of the rhizome rather than the tree as a central image for cultural theory.[1] Yet the Llangernyw Yew, estimated between 2,000 and 5,000 years old, and hopelessly entangled in centu-ries of diverse human and non-human culture, survives as a living real symbol of the ecosemiotic importance of arboreal-ity, a reminder of trees as a real cross between immanence

---

[1] Gilles Deleuze and Félix Guattari's *A Thousand Plateaus*, trans. Brian Massumi (Minneapolis: University of Minnesota Press, 1987), vol. 2 of their project *Capitalism and Schizophrenia*, celebrates in its opening section the experiential empirical-materialism of the rhi-zome (as in networks of grass roots) as opposed to the hierarchical tradition of arboreality in Western culture.

and transcendence. The tree at Llangernyw speaks for itself in many ways, but like Dr. Seuss' Lorax in an earlier imaginative age of environmentalism, this essay also will try to speak for the trees, with a voice rising from a medievalist *longue durée*.

The Llangernyw Yew may date back to the prehistoric Bronze Age, but the churchyard graves resting by it cluster around a church supposedly founded by a fifth-century Cornish saint, son of Constantine of Cornwall. Digain would have lived amid the deeply rooted continuities and adaptive confusions of sub-Roman West Britain, an Irish Sea world of early medieval native Christian culture.[2] People there identified with a mythical ancient Britain, and only later with Cymru, or the land of comrades, as if still in echo of their old citizenry in the Roman province, in resistance to the English label of "Welsh" or *alien* for the conquered natives. Historians have remarked on how perhaps only in the Byzantine world was there such rooted continuity of community from the Roman era.[3] Yet early medieval art in Wales suggests adaptability as well as continuity and enduring cosmopolitan contexts. In another yew-shaded churchyard, at Nevern (Nanhyfer) in Southwest Wales, overhanging the Nefern River's trout and salmon, austere early Christian stone monuments morph in design into the later "tree of life" intricacies of a 10th- or 11th-century Irish-style "Celtic cross" standing stone.

To let trees be trees, as it were, it helps to get out from under the postmodern critique of arboreality as hierarchical and thus bad, and to go back under the bushy Llangeryn and Nevern yews, as well as metaphorically into the rhizomatic intricracy of the Nevern "tree of life" stone cross. In fact, the living symbolism of a tree, both rooted and uprearing, marks the intersection of the immanent and transcendent, which the environmental philosopher Erazim Kohák describes as essential for authentic personal experience of the earth.[4] Kohák argues, channeling Martin Heidegger, that a healthy

[2] *Eastern Conwy Churches Survey, Church of St. Digain, Llangernyew*, http://www.cpat.demon.co.uk/projects/longer/churches/conwy/16869.htm.

[3] K.R. Dark, *Civitas to Kingdom: British Political Continuity 300-800* (Leicester: Leicester University Press, 1994).

[4] Erazim Kohák, *The Embers and the Stars: A Philosophical Inquiry into the Moral Sense of Nature* (Chicago: University of Chicago Press, 1987).

respect for the mysterious "other side" of anything or any-body's nature is as essential to avoiding objectification as appreciation of its immanence.[5] Trees remain an age-old symbol of the mysterious side of life, from their hidden reach within the earth and up into the sky, their rollicking non-geometric form, which always has a literal "other side," the non-human life that they hide in different dimensions and elements from microbes to bears, their frequent age beyond humans and most living things, to the empathy they engen-der in human cultures that still live within trees and off their fruit and oxygen, within megalopolitan matrices as well as mythological forests and vacation respites.

THE ARBOREAL AND THE HIERARCHICAL

Hierarchy justifiably bears a bad name in the modern West, and this is at the heart of the Deleuzean critique of the ar-boreal in the abstract. Originally the term derives from a Greek root associated in meaning with "rule by priests" and "leader of sacred rites." But as an abstract noun, *hierarchy* first came into use in the early medieval writings of that apophatic author whose name appropriately is itself a mys-tery, known today as the Pseudo-Dionysius. Most scholars hold the writer to have been a Syrian monastic or proto-monk in the fifth or sixth centuries, writing in a tradition attributed to St. Dionysius the Areopagite (better known in the West as St. Denys), an Athenian philosopher who be-came a disciple of St. Paul the Apostle. The visionary writer thus could well also be called the Christian Dionysius (as distinct from but as ecstatic in his own way as the pagan Di-onysius). But the "Pseudo" in his modern moniker fits well with his idea that human identity as well as the divine could not or should not be essentialized. There also is a cosmically mysterious side to the proper name (also known from pagan tradition). According to Christian tradition, the apostolic Dionysius encountered Paul when the latter was preaching to Classically learned Athenians at the Areopagus. Paul then (according to the Acts of the Apostles) glossed a line of Greek

---

[5] The "other side" of nature is developed as a theme in environmen-tal philosophy by Bruce V. Foltz in "Nature's Other Side: The Demise of Nature and the Phenomenology of Givenness," in *Rethinking Nature: Essays in Environmental Philosophy*, eds. Bruce V. Foltz and Robert Frodeman (Bloomington: University of Indiana Press, 2004), 330–342.

poetry by saying of God that "in Him we live and move and have our being" (Acts 17:28).

Appropriate to the writer's ecstatic name, the Christian Dionysian writings had a different take on "hierarchy" than the modern vertical power structure of oppression, the Deleuzean straw man in postmodernity's anti-tree campaign. In this earliest comprehensive writing about hierarchy, the term stands more for a network of divine energies or willings, in which every being, on every level of the network, had a direct connection with the divine, rather than an analogically fixed Scholastic or Darwinian conception of a genealogical "tree of life." The Dionysian hierarchy is apophatic in root and branch, meaning that it grows like a tree from "the other side of nature," at the crossroads of the transcendent and the immanent. It relates to the radically egalitarian yet transcendent vision of Paul, apparently so appealing to converts to Christianity in the Roman Empire and subsequently to the counter-culture of desert monasticism, that "there is neither Jew nor Gentile, there is neither slave nor free, there is neither male nor female," in the cosmic unity of Christ (Galatians 3:28). That vision was rooted in tree symbolism: The Tree of Life in the Book of Genesis, associated with the Cross, and ultimately with the tree whose leaves were for the healing of the nations in Revelation (22:2).

The Dionysian writings, with their hybrid rhizomatic-arboreal view of hierarchy, were translated in two venues of significance for the roots of Insular Transatlantic writing about trees: 1) by the early Irish nature writer Eriugena in his *Periphyseon* and 2) apparently by the author of the Middle English *Cloud of Unknowing*, himself often thought to be an East Midlands parson, perhaps, one can wonder whimsically, even a contemporary model for Chaucer's Parson in *The Canterbury Tales*. In both Eriugena's 9th-century nature writing (which paralleled in its approach to nature a number of early Irish Sea writings about Creation with apparent influence on Middle English literature), and in the late 14th century flowering of English literature to which the *Deonise Hid Divinite* (a translation of the Dionysian "Mystical Theology" text) contributed, apophatic hierarchy as well as trees figured significantly, and in ways at odds with the type of arboreal vertical hierarchy that in modern times understandably ticked off Deleuze and Guattari.

The Middle English version seems to emphasize affective love more in its indirect (via Latin) translation of the original Dionysius' Greek. But it follows the original tradition in emphasizing, citing Dionysius' other work on *The Hierarchies of Heaven*, that there can be a leading up of a ladder (as a carpentered image that also could be a climbing tree, for what in effect is really a kind of energy network or web) from things that are seen to the ineffable. That ladder leans above on the unknowable, the "other side" of nature, a "sky hook" that yet relates to the incarnationalism of the Creator assuming form in Creation. Medieval Christian writers symbolized the Mother of God as both an embodiment of this arboreal ladder between earth and heaven (typed by the angels in Jacob's vision dynamically ascending and descending) and the earthly house of the pillars of Divine Wisdom (referenced by Solomon), a living sign of the uncreated energies of Divine Wisdom integrating Creation and the Divine. In these interactive reciprocities, there is no essentialism to provide a basis for objectification, no Deleuzean sense of static and oppressive hierarchy, but rather a flowing sparkling and tingling of grace perfusing Creation with meaning. This is what made apophatic theology attractive to Jacques Derrida, and an analogue to his theory of deconstruction, even as he would not commit to its theism. In short, the medieval Tree of Life in the apophatic Dionysian sense of hierarchy (involving a dialogic materialism of personalism rather than a more abstract dialectical materialism) is pansemiotic, an all-meaningful network of life. It is the All Tree referenced by the Hiberno-Latin early medieval nature writer Eriugena, Maximus the Confessor, and John of Damascus, the Tree identified with the Logos (a word from Greek philosophy meaning variously "word," "harmony," "purpose," "reason," "principle," "narrative," "discourse," "story," and a term adapted in early Christianity for Christ or God incarnate). In the Damascene's terms, this is the Logos that thickens into Image: Here we sit in the branches as birds who sing, the *logoi* of the Logos, the words of the Word, or the harmonies of the harmonies, in an alternate translation.

TREES AND NATURAL LAW

The relation of the idea of hierarchy to notions of natural law undoubtedly raised the ire of Deleuze and Guattari in their negative identification of the arboreal with hierarchy. But it also raises the question of how Dionysian trees, as distinct from Deleuzean trees, would represent natural law. Apophatically, they would appear to do so in a bush-like manner, which again interweaves what modernity separated as rhizomatic and arboreal, through energy, rather than a matrix of analogy. The *logoi* are not merely archetypes or seeds but embodied meaningfulness, as organized in a cosmic syntax or chant, but they both shape identity and power its redemption in relationship, as information-energy more than a static essentialist core. If Scholasticism advocates *an-alogia entis*, in which being exists in analogy to fixed archetypes, then Dionysian apophaticism expresses *energeia entis*, an energy of being, akin to current notions of physics that see information-energy as basic to life, rather than atomistic energy. Natural law based in apophatic theology must be more mysterious, more experiential, and more a sparkle than a matrix, by comparison with that of the Scholastics.

Erazim Kohák in *The Embers and the Stars* suggests how the Ten Commandments can be interpreted in an apophatic-environmental mode, expressing a desire based in relationship rather than in lack and objectification. This can be symbolized by the bush-tree of Sinai, the burning bush identified by medieval Christians with the Mother of God, who encompassed the Creator while being encompassed by Him, yet was seen as typed by Jacob's ladder, too, with more verticality than an entangled bush. The Llangernyw Yew lacks a core and lives bush-like in sprouted offshoots in its ancient churchyard, and the Glastonbury thorn is a bush of many offshoots, although a type of hawthorn tree. According to tradition, that tree-bush grew from Joseph of Arimathea's planting of his staff in the ground at Glastonbury in apostolic times. It inspired legends enshrined in William Blake's "Jerusalem," sung at the end of the BBC proms each summer, as well as in the background of the Glastonbury Festival and Thomas Malory's rendering of the Grail legend. Such bushy tree and tree-ish bush hybridity in living-tree symbols raises the issue again of how trees have been reduced to vertical symbols only.

Even the family trees in the Bible, the genealogical glue of Genesis in particular, other Hebrew historical books, and the Christian gospels, elude modern notions of strict hierarchical oppressiveness. For one thing, they are mysteriously personal rather than abstractly rationalized in their life spans, chronology, and details, and trace ultimately back to Adam and Eve and beyond. They also include unlikely and non-hierarchical mixes of saints and sinners, including harlots and murderers among the ancestors of God in Christian tradition. They evoke in their connectivity nonetheless a sense of what the Haudenosaunee or Iroquois call the ethos of the seventh generation, experiencing one's life trajectory in intergenerational as well as in horizontal-cohort terms, again an intersection arguably of the rhizomatic and the arboreal. It's no coincidence in that sense that the Iroquois also revere a Tree of Life associated with Creation, related also to their white-pine Tree of Peace.

At the campus where I work, along the Susquehanna River, grows a white pine that is a "tree of peace" given by traditional leaders of the Haudenosaunee Confederacy or Six Nations. Also nearby on campus is a sculpture entitled *Seven Generations*, installed by the sculptor Frederick Franck in 1991. Its plaque reads: "In all our deliberations we must be mindful of the impact of our decisions on the next seven generations," referencing the Iroquois "great law." The sculpture features metal frames designed to represent simultaneously either each generation looking forward through the next, or each looking back through the preceding generations. Both the landscape and the viewer-participants become living parts of the sculpture, because of the way it is designed. But only six generations survive in the sculpture today. According to campus lore, the "seventh" fell prey to an issue of cultural translation after it was erected in the 1990s with the support of Native Americans. The seventh generation was sculpted in the form of an embryo. It disappeared during the night after pro-choice activists on campus had criticized its symbolism. This conflict over portrayals of the hierarchical arboreal notion of the "seventh generation" ethos (with its "family tree" assumptions) underlines both the problem of different cultural interpretations of arboreal hierarchy and the power of such imagery to evoke embodied feeling.

Our campus in the Susquehanna Valley stands in a center of the ancient Eastern Woodlands of America, which disappeared in a spurt of nineteenth-century lumbering that clear-cut almost all the region. Yet the symbolic importance of the forest and trees lived on, in particular to the Haudenosaunee, the dominant Native culture in the watershed in the mid-eighteenth century, before their military confinement in the early American republic to their current national lands in upstate New York and Canada. In intervening years the physical forests have enjoyed a comeback of sorts, thanks to the legacy of Gifford Pinchot and the Pennsylvania state forests, under the umbrella also of Theodore Roosevelt's national efforts, going back to his initial work in the Adirondacks, which were inspired in part by James Fenimore Cooper's fictional ghost stories about the Eastern Woodlands in his Leatherstocking Tale series. Today the forests are becoming ever more a part of the felt culture of increasingly diverse communities in the Susquehanna watershed. This is evidenced in recent controversy over the effect of fracking on wooded areas like the nearby Loyalsock State Forest. Long ago that tract itself was mainly clear cut, in an earlier era of resource extraction. But now this green wood has come back, and in some ways again is definitional of the area.

THE GREEN WOOD AND SUSTAINABILITY OF THE IMAGINATION

James Fenimore Cooper, in writing America's first environmental novel, *The Pioneers*, in 1823, shaped a sense of the American "green world" that he continued to evoke, as a literary ghost of the Eastern Woodlands, throughout his Leatherstocking Tales. Not only did his evocation of the primordial forest inspire young Theodore Roosevelt as a budding conservationist, it also continued to inspire generations of Americans growing up in the early 20th-century Scouting movement and other outdoor activities, supporting conservationism with a sense of the loss of American Paradise. Cooper's daughter Susan Fenimore Cooper, one of America's earliest nature writers and a precursor to Henry David Thoreau, exemplified in her writings the vision of shaping an American Arcadia to replace the lost green wood. Her writings evoke the potential of garden communities in which trees could be both rhizomatic and arboreal, and support and symbolize the type of entwining communitarian and localist social justice that she fostered in her nun-like philanthropy of founding and directing an orphanage, organizing a hospital, and writing meticulously of the natural world around her home in a way that nurtured a local ethos of conservation. In her essay on "Village Improvement Societies," Susan Cooper wrote of her vision of tree-focused American villages.[6] This emerged from her view of the human role on Earth as that of gardener, steward, and priest of transfigurative communion, not a presumptuous would-be creator. She saw Americans living under tree branches and among their roots and trunks, as part of a transcendence woven into immanence, needed for us to approach the mystery of what the

[6] Susan Fenimore Cooper, "Village Improvement Societies," in *Essays on Nature and Landscape*, eds. Rochelle Johnson and Daniel Patterson (Athens: University of Georgia Press, 2002), 64–77.

Declaration of Independence refers to as "the laws of Nature and Nature's God." Speaking of the record of the creation of trees in Genesis, that "the Lord God made to grow every tree that is pleasant to the sight," she wrote,

> This simple phrase, taken in connection with all its sub-lime relations of time and place, has a gracious tender-ness, a compassionate beneficence of detail which moves the heart deeply; all the delight which the trees of the wood have afforded to men, independently of their uses; the many peaceful homes they have overshadowed; the many eyes they have gladdened; all the festal joys of the race in which their branches have waved, seem to crowd the mind in one graceful picture, and force from our lips the familiar invocation, 'O all ye green things upon earth, bless ye the Lord; praise him, and magnify him forever.'[7]

Eriugena's "tree of life," and the analogous Celtic Otherworld landscapes that influenced Middle English texts such as *The Canterbury Tales, Sir Gawain and the Green Knight*, and *Le Morte Darthur*, seem to morph by Elizabethan times into the "green world" of the green wood, not surprising given the cultural and biological magnetism of trees, as well as the way in which disappearing forest in the British Isles was becom-ing more a geography of imagination. But as suggested by the experience of the Haudenosaunee and the literary legacy of the Coopers, such arboreal geography of imagination could be tenacious. "Ecosemiosphere" is one way to describe the cultural life of the Eastern Woodlands, drawing on eco-semiotics as developed at Tartu and Copenhagen. Just as a semiosphere is a bubble of meaning in an environment (human or non-human), so an ecosemiosphere closely en-twines multiple semiospheres within a particularly meaning-ful ecosystem or region.

By championing the "immaterial" side of nature in com-munication and relationship, ecosemiotics follows Charles S. Peirce in highlighting ecology as the meaningful relationship of sign-making, the cross of the arboreal and rhizomatic, in which signs are embodied feelings with environmental con-notations. Such a semiotic view encouraged the emphasis on empathy that from Peirce's day based the critique of what

---

[7] Susan Fenimore Cooper, "Introduction to *The Rhyme and Reason*," in *Essays on Nature and Landscape*, 31 [24–44].

Gregory Bateson and others highlighted as an individualistic Anglo-American emphasis on Darwinian natural selection from the standpoint of organism rather than ecosystem.[8] What's at stake may not be so much the arboreal vs. the rhizomatic as one kind of tree symbolism vs. another: the Darwinian tree of life with teleological pedigrees, growing out of a context of British colonialism and expanding capitalism, and the tree as a cross of the transcendent and immanent, understandable in today's information age as identifiable with Peirce's "immaterial" sign processes as formative of nature. The philosopher of mind Evan Thompson argues that biology and ecology today require a sense of nature that is more homologic than analogic.[9] Paradoxically, ancient tree symbolism of transcendental rootedness resonates more with that current sensibility than the biological tree of life in the nineteenth century, which is challenged by ever-stranger speculations in physics on the multiverse and quantum entanglement. Yggdrasil was always at home in a multiverse. The non-geometric strangeness and multidimensionality of each tree offers its own symbolic quantum entanglement.

Even the celebrated "entangled bank" at the end of Charles Darwin's *The Origin of Species* really only offers a brief imaginative glimpse of landscape, overshadowed by the analogous use of the scene for contemplating the laws behind it, traced to a watchmaker-like Creator. The Llangernyw Yew in real life affords by contrast a not-so-utilitarian experience, of an ecosemiotic symbol that is real, enclustered with human culture for millennia. This can evoke contemplation that leads not to reflection on a matrix of analogous laws, but phenomenologically to experience of the relational entanglement of story, human and non-human, in a more personal and experiential way than the *analogia entis* that continues to limit contemporary Western approaches to the environment.

---

[8] See, for example, Timothy Ingold, "Three in one: how an ecological approach can obviate the distinctions between body, mind and culture," in *Imagining nature: practices of cosmology and identity*, eds. A Roepstorff and N. Bub (Denmark: Aarhus University Press), 40–55.
[9] Evan Thompson, *Mind in Life* (Cambridge: Belknap/Harvard University Press, 2007), 195.

CONCLUSION: LET TREES BE TREES AND A THOUSAND LORAXES GROW

Trees have been posited as a postmodern embarrassment. Deleuze and Guattari in the opening of *A Thousand Plateaus* condemned trees as hierarchical and not immanent enough, in a word transcendental, not rhizomatic but arboreal. Yet to Mediterranean and European pre-moderns trees were *both* transcendent and immanent, rhizomatic and arboreal. They saw trees more as trees, with real roots and branches connecting micro-ecosystems. Deleuze and Guattari, as Peter Hallward noted, were in some ways close to the early medieval cosmology of Eriugena, who held nature to be a theophany. For D&G, as my students call them, nature was an ecophany. But in eliminating the transcendent, they paradoxically missed the mystery of a real tree, the substance of which they still pursued in spirit in their rhizome and bodies without organs. Heidegger had noted that philosophy has not been yet able to let a tree actually *be* a tree, although typically he then went on himself to do the same.[10] Now we are left with a technophany of dark ecology, symbolized arboreally in Singapore's super trees, the manmade metallic giant trees prefiguring ziggurats of the 21st century.

But in early medieval literature and art, we have examples of trees allowed to be trees imaginatively and cosmically—taking the term cosmic in its Greek meaning of beauty and adornment in the environmental world, and implying a pattern of non-human mystery with in effect a life of its own, though interwoven with human shaping of the beautiful through *techné* or craft. In the Old English poem *The Dream of the Rood*, in one view the tree is bejeweled and light-filled, in another cut down, a victim of colonial oppression. Yet the tree is given a voice and agency and a teaching role for humans, as is the creation that weeps at the crucifixion of the Creator God on the Earth. In the early Irish narratives of *The Voyage of St. Brendan*, trees are given voice by birds singing the liturgical hours. In Icelandic Eddic literature we read of Yggdrasil, the cosmic tree, which contains different worlds in its branches and roots, and upon which a squirrel runs between a dragon at the roots and the eagle at its top. Then there is the battle of the trees in a poem attributed to Taliesin.

[10] See Martin Heidegger, *What is Called Thinking?* (New York: Harper Perennial, 1976), 38–44.

In Malory we have the forest of adventure and woods around Glastonbury and Avalon where survivors seek solace. Those were landscapes of the green world, literary successor to the Celtic Otherworld, framed by trees, transplanted into Anglo-American imagination, melding with Native American tree lore. The Celtic Otherworld itself was a stand-in for the biblical Paradise in which early created trees and plants dwelled peaceably with humans under the branches and above the roots of the All Tree referenced in early Greek translations of Genesis.

Perhaps the most memorable tree symbolism from medieval Ireland, besides sacred trees of its monasteries, is St. Columba's Cuilebad, or liturgical fan, a leaf from an otherworldly tree, similar to the fruit from the Tree of Life brought back by Saint Euphrosynus the Cook. But the spelling out of the name of that fan in the Book of Ballymote suggests the relic was a name for wheel-writing in ogam, and so a symbol linking natural object to art and writing. As noted earlier, St. Maximus the Confessor in the seventh century similarly described the biblical Tree of Life as the Logos including singing *logoi* of creation in its branches, or the words of the Word, harmonies of the Harmony, a theme picked up by Eriugena.

The difference between Columba's fan and the Singapore super trees is that one arguably is the symbol of the coming together of heaven and earth, and the other of human mastery over material elements through conceptual analogy. Columba's fan is more reminiscent of the singing golden bird in the golden tree of William Butler Yeats' "Sailing to Byzantium." The early medieval symbol arose from a culture whose heyday in the era of the Book of Kells paralleled Byzantium's time as center of an early Christianity at the intersection of Classical Greek and Hebrew views of nature. The Tree as Cross formed a symbol of the intersection of the transcendent and immanent in the personal, in the person of the Creator made physical. This tree entwined for early medieval Christians the experience of Moses' burning bush and the vine of the gospel Logos and *logoi*, aspects of both Classical Greek and biblical Hebrew cosmology. Heaven and earth entwine in the branches and roots of such treeness in a way neither fully pantheistic nor panentheistic.

Pavel Florensky and Sergei Bulgakov shaped the early medieval intersection of the Holy Cross or Holy Tree into a modern sophic ecology. Highlighting connections of the Hebrew notion of Divine Wisdom and the Greek sense of Logos, they defined Divine Sophia as that which, as Bulgakov wrote, "shines in the world as the primordial purity and beauty of the universe, in the loveliness of a child and in the gorgeous enchantment of a swaying flower, in the beauty of a starry sky and a flaming sunrise."[11] Sophia spanned the divine and the created, in created form symbolized by the Mother of God. We see echoes of this old experiential way of experiencing the pansemiotic personalized immanent-yet-transcendent Earth, of "magnifying" a green world, even in 15th-century Robin Hood ballads, where life beneath the green wood is associated with devotion to "Our Lady." So, too, Classical dryads were both feminine and dendric avatars of Earth, similar to our current Gaia theory, illustrating how arboreal cosmic views incorporated female as well as male elements.

When we think of sustainability as including imagination, in that which enables us to endure and endures us on the earth,[12] trees remain the go-to symbol for both rootedness and branching out, Deleuze and Guattari aside. Environmental phenomenologist David Wood noted in his essay "Trees and Truth, or Why We Are Really All Druids" that trees living or dead still shape our lives and often form our houses and furniture and landscapes. It is in one sense right to criticize Darwinian evolution, he argues, in that human beings have not evolved out of living in trees. We still live within them—physically and imaginatively, root and branch, leaf and page, virtual or not.[13] Like the Lorax from that earlier imaginative era of environmentalism—almost as distant to today's I-culture as the Middle Ages—eco-poets can still speak for the trees, when humbly seeing them as both real and symbolic, not merely as objects, not as one or the other.

---

[11] Cited in Pavel Florensky, *The Pillar and the Ground of Truth: An Essay in Orthodox Theodicy in Twelve Letters*, trans. Boris Jakim (Princeton: Princeton University Press, 2004), 83.

[12] On imagination as the fourth leg of sustainability (usually now defined in environmental, economic, and social terms), see Leslie Paul Thiele, *Sustainability* (Cambridge: Polity Press, 2013), 4–5.

[13] David Wood, "Trees and Truth, or Why We Are Really All Druids," in *Re-Thinking Nature*, ed. Foltz and Frodeman, 32–43.

FLUID

James Smith

Thus it is that the mutability of the present is a topic that is always old, yet ever new, old to those who through experience or reflection learnt it long ago, new to those who, awakened by experience or admonished by teaching, are just beginning for the first time to know it now.

Hugh of Saint-Victor, *De Vanitate Mundi*

Living under liquid modern conditions can be compared to walking in a minefield: everyone knows an explosion might happen at any moment and in any place, but no one knows when the moment will come and where the place will be. On a globalized planet, that condition is universal – no one is exempt and no one is insured against its consequences.

Zygmunt Bauman, *Liquid Modernity*

To flow is to strive against inertia, to spread forth, to become diluted by the myriad eddies of life, to become enriched by new influx. To flow is to be lost, to rush through life, to be dashed upon unfamiliar resistance, to feel turmoil within. As the pre-Socratic philosopher Heraclitus reminds us, every-thing flows (*panta rhei*).[1] These dynamics form a bond of historical specificities merged with material legacies across time, for the fluidity of creativity, composition, and dyna-mism must ever inspire and unsettle in equal measure. The moral anxieties expressed by Hugh of Saint-Victor in the epi-gram above are both distinctly medieval in moral register and redolent of modern anxieties expressed by Zygmunt Bauman in the second epigraph: they explore a fear that changeability is paradoxically unexpected and inevitable haunts us all. Life flows by at a pace that is both endlessly unsettling and enduringly typical. This paper flows through the fluid anxieties of medieval moral life, and empties itself into modern vicissitudes. It seeks to expose a manifest ecol-ogy of the inhuman, a moveable alterity of time and chance that encapsulates human life and yet endlessly entangles it. As Ovid termed it in the *Metamorphoses*, time is *tempus edax rerum*, the devourer of things; its vast maw both the entrance into dissolution and the digestion of old into the endless new.[2] In a medieval context, temporal transition was sur-rounded by, set within, a smooth celestial eternity; time roiled within endless calm. In this discussion, I explore the rendering of the endless dissolution and reconstitution of things through the popular evocation of fluid properties, the shaping of an ecological *habitus* revealed within medieval thought and implied within modern thought through a strong vein of discourse.

To say that life is fluid is to forge a link that immediately breaks the chain of signification expected of metaphorical representation. It is in fact an environment, a setting for hu-man striving, defined by endless and fraught transaction with scales and priorities of alienating impersonality.[3] De-

---

[1] As claimed by Plato in the *Cratylus*, 401d, in Harold North Fowler, ed., *Plato: Cratylus, Parmenides, Greater Hippias, Lesser Hippias*, Loeb Classical Library (Cambridge: Harvard University Press, 1926).

[2] Publius Ovidius Naso, *Metamorphoses*, XV: 234–236: http://www.thelatinlibrary.com/ovid/ovid.met15.shtml.

[3] And yet it is not, as Stacy Alaimo has claimed, a symptom of a word "drained of its blood" by constant appropriation and misuse. It is a space for humans defined by the very vibrancy that has been lost in the transition from the Latin etymology of environment to the lexical revenant we encounter today. See *Bodily Natures: Science, Environ-*

spite this ambivalence, this space is generative: just as it devours, so too does it create. It is no coincidence that evocation of fluid metaphor brings with it an upwelling feeling of synergy, like a barely remembered dream of form emerging from a scarce-imagined conceptual shadow. In the terminology of Hans Blumenberg a fluid context can, and does, bring about *absolute metaphor*, a process beyond connecting the dots of conceptuality, a process that composes and creates. More than a series of codified interactions between signifiers and signifieds, the space shaped by absolute metaphor is an environs within which ideas are born, teem, interact, unsettle, and grow.[4] Blumemberg offers us a world in which inspirations are never exhausted, but continue to multiply and compose, a catalyic sphere from which the universe of concepts continually renews itself, without thereby converting and exhausting this founding reserve".[5]

If we apply this notion to the fluid ecology of the inhuman, we gain an insight into practices of sense-making stimulated by the prolific motions of our metaphorical wellspring, the experience of environment through the senses, and in endless interactions with a complex ecological perspective. Like the 'clearing' that Martin Heidegger imagined as the home of *dasein*, of *being there*, we occupy the observer position amid the seething generative force in which meaning is constantly born and the inhumanity of environment is constantly inscrutable.[6] Here, in our dwelling place, we view

---

ment, and the Material Self (Bloomington: Indiana University Press, 2010), 1–2.

[4] "By providing a point of orientation," Blumenberg claimed, "the content of absolute metaphors determines a particular attitude or conduct; they give structure to a world": Hans Blumenberg, *Paradigms for a Metaphorology* (Ithaca: Cornell University Press, 2010), 14.

[5] Blumenberg, *Paradigms for a Metaphorology*, 4. Blumenberg is an apt citation for a thesis on medieval thought, for his work as a medievalist was a key component of his development of *Paradigms for a Metaphorology*. His interrogation of space and metaphor is particularly apt. For a key example, see his book *Shipwreck with Spectator: Paradigm of a Metaphor for Existence* (Cambridge: M.I.T. Press, 1997), a text based heavily on medieval case material.

[6] "In the midst of beings as a whole an open place occurs. There is a clearing, a lighting . . . . Only this clearing grants and guarantees to us humans a passage to those beings that we ourselves are not, and

the expanses of possibilities, the stark contrast of limitations, and the overall immutability of the space that defines them. When the fluid content of this paper enters our consideration, we see that the turbulent stage for life is not a static clearing, but an ever-shifting series of engagements and entanglements. This is an affective mixture of communions and alienations, comforts and insecurities, as Gregory J. Seigworth and Melissa Gregg propose:

> Affect marks a body's *belonging* to a world of encounters or; a body's belonging to a world of encounters but also, in *non-belonging*, through all those far sadder (de)compositions of mutual in-compossibilities. Always there are ambiguous or "mixed" encounters that impinge or extrude for worst or for better, but (most usually) in-between.[7]

This essay considers the ambiguities of fluid as a mixed encounter, as manifested within medieval moral anxieties, and within the context of modern concerns.[8] Through the formation of ecological spaces that negotiate complex interplays between fluctuating temporalities, moral states, fears, and opportunities, this essay generates a form of ecological thought in which, as Timothy Morton has observed, "the more you know, the more entangled you realize you are, and the more open and ambiguous everything becomes."[9] The anxiety of moral life on either end of an orderly 'solid' modernity reveals a startling fact: that we—the *we* formed by the discourse between medieval and modern thought-worlds— *fear* the inhuman and mutable. The argument begins, as does this tale of fear, opportunity, and ecological entanglement, with pre-modern mourning for the passing of things.

---

access to the being that we ourselves are": Martin Heidegger, *Poetry, Language, Thought*, trans. Albert Hofstadter (New York: Harper and Row, 1971), 53.

[7] Gregory J. Seigworth and Melissa Gregg, "An Inventory of Shimmers," in *The Affect Theory Reader*, eds. Gregory J. Seigworth and Melissa Grigg (Durham: Duke University Press, 2010), 2 [1–28].

[8] Or equally a trans-corporeal encounter, the "interconnections, interchanges, and transits" between human and non-human proposed by Stacy Alaimo, *Bodily Natures*, 2.

[9] Timothy Morton, *The Ecological Thought* (Cambridge: Harvard University Press, 2010), 17.

TURBULENCE AND TRANQUILITY: TRAVERSING THE MEDIEVAL
MORAL OCEAN

I stick fast in the mire of the deep
and there is no sure standing.
I am come into the depth of the sea,
and a tempest hath overwhelmed me.[10]
Psalm 68

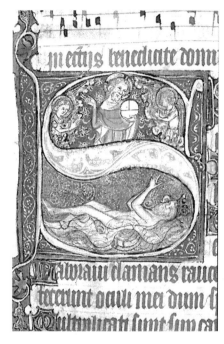

Figure 1: Historiated Initial of Psalm 68 ((S)aluum), from 14th c. Psalter of Queen Philippa, British Library MS. Harley 2899, f. 53.

For medieval thinkers, the world flowed for good and for ill;
the world shaped and thwarted the projected form of a hu-

---

[10] "infixus sum in limo profundi et non possum consistere veni in
profundum aquarum et flumen operuit me": from the Douay-
Rheims translation of the Latin Vulgate Bible (http://www.drbo.
org/).

man life. Fundamental patterns of vital motion, the very forces that drove the cosmos, were the same forces that epitomized the flaws of temporality. The response within the human heart? Anguish. "Why do we love you, O World, as you flee from us?" entreated Alcuin of York in his poem *O Mea Cella*.[11] Alcuin's ardent allegoresis of the world as addressable dissolves instantly into a torrent of inhuman motion. The answer? Contempt. In the twelfth century, Hugh of Saint-Victor described the temporal world, with all that is in it, as "flood water sweeping past, whose inundations and changing currents—whether we compare them to a flood that covers everything or to a mighty sea—are very like reality."[12] Regarding the human heart, Hugh admonishes the reader to remember that "All things pass and flow and not a thing subsists under the sun, so that the sentence is fulfilled: *vanity of vanities, vanity of vanities, all is vanity.*"[13]

The inevitable and complex interplay of temporalities inherent in this *vanitas* created the queer complexities recently explored by Caroline Dinshaw in *How Soon is Now*, but also sets the stage for a space of striving and anxiety occupied by individuals seeking to find strategies to overcome or contextualize their situation.[14] The diverse and chaotic temporalities encountered within the sea of the world were both an individual and collective experience, their navigation a confusing mixture of reactions. Time, for these navigators, was self-contradictory and chaotic by its very nature: the goal of its experience was the transcendence of its effects.[15] Rather

---

[11] "cur te fugitivum, mundus, amamus?": http://www.thelatinlibrary.com/alcuin/cella.shtml.

[12] Hugh of St. Victor, "Noah's Ark III," *De Vanitate Mundi*, in *Hugh of St. Victor: Selected Spiritual Writings / Translated by a Religious of C.S.M.V., with an Introduction by Aelred Squire, O.P.* (London: Faber, 1962), 175–176.

[13] "Hugh of Saint Victor: Theology and Interiority," in Ineke van't Spijker, ed., *Fictions of the Inner Life: Religious Literature and Formation of the Self in the Eleventh and Twelfth Centuries* (Turnhout: Brepols, 2004), 119–120.

[14] See Caroline Dinshaw, *How Soon is Now? Medieval Texts, Amateur Readers, and the Queerness of Time* (Durham: Duke University Press, 2010).

[15] Thus the fear and the opportunity vis-à-vis fluid ecologies that I explore in this essay. As Dinshaw has suggested in the case of temporality, however, seeing this fluid space as a "time/not time" prop-

than an austere and didactic space of monolithic disorder, I instead propose a complex network of porous and mutual entanglements that medieval thinkers bemoaned and despaired of, and yet sought to harness for the purpose of self-edification.[16] The contempt felt by medieval, and particularly monastic, thinkers towards the world was not as simple as antipathy, but instead a galvanizing and motive distrust that imbued the spirit with the will to engage and not to drown.

The *vanitas* perceived by Hugh within the passing of the world constitutes a human affective response to the molestation of medieval moral life by what Jane Bennett might call an 'impersonal affect' of fluidity. In the treacherous flux, Benett's "subsistent world of non-human vitality" emerges, and yet it is not a vitality that medieval people could be content with.[17] The fluidity of temporal life swept up the soul in a complex web of interactions, and yet such a participation carried risk. In a medieval intellectual world encapsulated by a shifting and swirling maelstrom, matter had a disturbing agency.[18] As Augustine put it in *De Doctrina Christiana*, the world was to be used as a vehicle of travel, not to be enjoyed.[19] It was somewhat disturbing when the world used you. Through myriad pushings and pullings, buffetings and fluxes, the motions of the medieval world propelled not only human life, but the mobile cosmos on a grand scale.

In his twelfth-century *De Contemptu Mundi*, Bernard of Cluny evoked the trope of the fugitive world in a powerful display of spiritual pathos. The cycle of impermanence con-

---

osition where a manifold chaos is simple in its opposition to a solid order negates the vitality and complexity of medieval moral life.

[16] Tim Ingold suggests that "the organism is not limited by the skin. *It, too, leaks*": Tim Ingold, "Point, Line and Counterpoint: From Environment to Fluid Space," in Alain Berthoz and Yves Christen, eds., *Neurobiology of "Umwelt": How Living Beings Perceive the World, Research and Perspectives in Neurosciences* (Berlin: Springer, 2009), 153.

[17] Jane Bennett, *Vibrant Matter: A Political Ecology of Things* (Durham: Duke University Press, 2010), xi–xiii.

[18] An agency highlighted in particular by Caroline Walker Bynum through the often-disruptive materiality of Christian material objects. See her book *Christian Materiality: An Essay on Religion in Late Medieval Europe* (Cambridge: M.I.T. Press, 2011).

[19] Augustine, *De Doctrina Christiana*, Book 1, Chapters 3–5: http://www.newadvent.org/fathers/12021.htm.

tinued uninterrupted *ab initio mundi*, and would endure until the Day of Judgement. The space between the birth and end of worldly turbulence, the alpha and omega of temporal motion, served as a constant counterexample for those steeped in the mores of monastic spirituality, and a space within which the entangled struggled to preserve a clear ob-server position in a chaotic vortex of ecology:

> See how the whirling courses of things hasten away, like streams of water. The world's glory has fallen and fled and vanished in the cycle of days . . . . Its position is un-fixed, its status is unstable. It goes and it returns, like the sea, now bad and tomorrow even worse.[20]

Within Bernard's words, we apprehend the mixed encounter described by Seigworth and Gregg, a deep and violent emo-tional incompossibility. *De Contemptu Mundi* reveals sad-ness for the non-belonging of humanity in an ecology of deeply alienating inhumanity, and yet a paradoxical and in-finitely more sad illusion of belonging. For Bernard, the cru-elty of the world was indicated not only by its alienating qualities, but by the endless false friendships that were the transactions of human life. *De Vanitate Mundi* forms an ex-treme in a continuum of medieval opinions. Aelred of Rie-vaulx, in contrast, argued that "among non-sentient beings, a kind of love of companionship comes to light, since not one of them is left alone, but each is created and conserved in a kind of society of its own class."[21] Bernard saw the strife, and not the unity, at work within ecology. The world was beautiful and dynamic, and through its color and manifold enchantments it hid the ugly face of change. It was a space of beguiling innocence hiding endless fickleness. What seemed at one moment to be calm and inviting in its tranquillity could and would be agitated to violent motion, often in the blink of an eye.

Lady Natura of Alan of Lille's twelfth-century *De Planctu Naturae* proclaimed that "at my mere will and wish [the

---

[20] *Scorn for the World: Bernard of Cluny's De contemptu mundi: The Latin Text with English Translation and an Introduction*, trans. Ronald E. Pepin (East Lansing: Michigan State University Colleagues Press, 1991), Book 1.71.

[21] *Aelred of Rievaulx: Spiritual Friendship*, trans. Lawrence C. Brace-land (Collegeville: Cistercian Publications, 2010), 1:54, 65–66.

world] is now vexed into the wrath of the storm, now returns to the peace of tranquillity, now, borne aloft by its swelling pride, rises to the likeness of a mountain, now is leveled out into a smooth plain."[22] Turbulence was natural within medieval morality—the *rota fortunae* was ever spinning—and yet its absence was of divine importance. The cruelty of life was that it required motion to exist, and yet brought about the dissolution of human integrity by the very same motion. Monastics felt this conflict keenly, and sought to warn others against it. Hugh of Saint-Victor is particularly strident in his warning to all who dwell within the sea of the world, and yet we get the sense that he is merely the spectator of a disaster inevitably unfolding before him:

> Poor wretches, what will become of you in this sea? Why did you put your trust in that deceptive calm? . . . O unhappy wretched men, see how swiftly your joy has been changed, and into what sorry plight your life has fallen. Once, in your foolish rejoicing, you found amusement in the fishes of the sea. Now, when you are shipwrecked and miserably cast away, they receive you as their food.[23]

The clarity and tranquillity of water at rest contrasts sharply and yet emerges in dialectic interplay with the fury and commotion of roiling waves. By constantly highlighting the danger and turbulent impermanence of worldly life, monastic writers created a space that suggested a simpler, purer, and stiller world that existed beyond it. For a medieval imagining, the waters that propelled human journeys through the ocean-forge of moral life contained an inherent and ongoing juxtaposition of a limpid morality of stilled and tranquil peace coupled with a roiling mass of confusion and strife. "You flow and you grow, you run down and you are engulfed," continues Hugh in a melancholy tone, "O stream that fails not, O watercourse never still, O whirlpool never sated!"[24] He recalls the divinely ordained punitive might of

---

[22] Douglas M. Moffatt, trans., *Alain of Lille [Alanus de Insulis], d. 1202, The Complaint of Nature* (North Haven: Archon Books, 1972); http://www2.kenyon.edu/projects/margin/alain.htm.

[23] Hugh of St. Victor, "Noah's Ark III," *De Vanitate Mundi*, 161.

[24] Noah's Ark III, *De Vanitate Mundi*, 171.

worldly life, of a disorder ordained by a wrathful God who "is mighty and strong, as a storm of hail: a destroying whirlwind, as the violence of many waters overflowing, and sent forth upon a spacious land."[25] The Flood of Genesis, it seems, is ever barely in check.

Hugh of Saint-Victor also proclaimed that "whatever is subject to birth, whatever involves the debt of mortality, that does insatiable death gulp down, it never ceases to consume the one and ensnare the other, or to engulf them both. The present is always passing on, the future always following; and, since the continuity is unbroken, there is a belief that this is the permanent condition of things."[26] The intellectual environment inhabited by the self-reflexive medieval thinker was both a place of belonging, and a place of endless alienation. To be born into this world was to incur a debt of permanence so anomalous to turbulence that life itself became a battle against entropy.[27] The storm of life, according to Hugh, was the result of the inconstant human heart, of the storm whipped up by intemperance. This was an inevitable motion, and yet potential remained for navigation through knowledge and technique, as Grover Zinn explains:

> At the outset of the treatise *De archa Noe* Hugh of St Victor recounts the occasion that gave rise to a conversation that led ultimately to the writing of the treatise. One day, Hugh says, he was answering questions put to him by his fellow regular canons, when discussion became focused on the "instability and restlessness" of the human heart. Implored by his brothers in religion to show the cause of this instability and, furthermore, to teach them if it could be cured "by any skill [arte] or by the practice of some discipline [laboris cuius libet exercitatione]."[28]

---

[25] "ecce validus et fortis Domini sicut impetus grandinis turbo confringens sicut impetus aquarum multarum inundantium et emissarum super terram spatiosam": Isaias 28:2, from the Douay-Rheims translation of the Latin Vulgate.

[26] Hugh of St. Victor, "Noah's Ark III," *De Vanitate Mundi*, 171–172.

[27] Within this battle was the *modus operandi* for opportunity within fluid ecology: before time could be overcome and its effects ameliorated, it was first necessary to move through it, to sail across it and to understand its localized conditions.

[28] Grover A. Zinn, "Minding Matter: Materia and the World in the Spirituality and Theology of Hugh of St. Victor," in Nancy Van-

This discipline, for monastics, stemmed from strict self-fashioning in the face of catastrophic fluidity. The ocean formed a moveable and multivalent stage for the drama of moral life, a road through the trials of Christian striving to the safe port of salvation. In the case of Hugh and his fellow Victorines, the discipline is ship-building, a method of harnessing the world as vehicle of travel. Christ and his sacrifice had made the negotiation of fluid life possible, a guiding hand at the helm. To stop motion would be to stop the transition of things, necessitating a stratagem dependent upon fluidity and turbulence, and yet designed to ameliorate its violent effects: edification matched with impermanence.[29]

The eleventh-century Benedictine theologian Guibert of Nogent claimed in his biography that "whenever the spirit no longer resists the flesh, the substance of the unhappy soul is eaten and wasted away by pleasure. A man who finds himself engulfed by raging waters is soon pulled to the bottom: so is one's judgement sucked down from the mouth of the well into the abyss of perversion."[30] The ocean of the world was thus a turbulent interstitial zone of trial and temptation. Fear of drowning motivated, hope of overcoming motivated. A commodious representation of the imagined mutability and opportunity of worldly life, the storm-tossed ocean provided danger and opportunity to the Christian: a danger of succumbing and an opportunity to rise above such temporal squalls. The process of moral life was a constant wrangling with the entropic/generative effects of Ovid's *tempus edax rerum*, as Peter of Celle suggests in this allegorical motif:

> As long as reason slumbered the barque of conscience in the world was shaken by the troughs of the sea, so that

Deusen and Cary J. Nederman, eds., *Mind Matters: Studies Of Medieval and Early-Modern Intellectual History In Honour Of Marcia Colish* (Turnhout: Brepols, 2009), 47–48 [47–68].

[29] As Steven Mentz discusses in his shipwreck essay (in this volume, and also in a forthcoming monograph), the construction of a "ship" leads to the endless possibility of shipwreck, an endlessly precarious and yet mobile position that provides the risk of death and of opportunity.

[30] *A Monk's Confession: The Memoirs of Guibert of Nogent*, trans. Paul J. Archambault (University Park: The Pennsylvania State University Press, 1996), 5.

> the prow of leading counsel was buffeted by the blows of carnal impulses, and the stern of reasoned judgement was dashed in a collision with dangerous rocks, that is, temptations which rise up frequently. The whole perimeter of the soul was spun around in a single gyration into a deep failure.[31]

At no point does Peter suggest that navigation is impossible, but the very *act* of navigation in the motion-driven realm of diverse temporal eddies requires movement. True stillness existed only in divinity or in a situation becalmed by divine intervention, and motion was necessary and normative. It was not desirable that motion was normative, but this was the state of things in a postlapsarian world. The challenge, as John Scotus Eriugena once described it, was to be aware of the rocks and the squalls, but to embrace them as the ultimate challenge of moral erudition:

> Let us spread our sails, then, and set out to sea. For Reason, not inexperienced in these waters . . . shall speed our course: indeed she finds it sweeter to exercise her skill in the hidden straights of the Ocean of divinity than idly to bask in the smooth and open waters where she cannot display her power.[32]

The mixed and trans-corporeal encounter that was the medieval Sea of the World gave medieval moral life both a punishment for the transgression of ideal order in the Fall, and an opportunity for travel with, in, and through the fluid inhumanity surrounding humanity. Rather than an abject and chaotic foil to an idealised and moralistic edifice of medieval thought, we can glimpse a true exercise of intellectual discipline. This was not a disembodied intellect-over-nature form of discipline, but a cooperation and collaboration with the other interconnected entities that made up the ecology of life and time. It was the prick of anguish at the disorder of emotion surrounding human life that compelled the seeker to

---

[31] Peter of Celle, "On Conscience," in *Peter of Celle: Selected Works*, trans. Hugo Feiss (Kalamazoo: Cistercian Publications, 1987), 58 [167–168].

[32] John Scotus Eriugena, as cited in Bernard McGinn, "Ocean and Desert as Symbols of Mystical Absorption in the Christian Tradition," *Journal of Religion* 74 (1994): 163 [155–181].

learn the carpentry of the intellect necessary to shape con-
text-appropriate adaptations. The fluid ecology was not the
ultimate destination of human life, nor was it the proper object of love; it was the medium by which a good life could be
negotiated one small move at a time, individually and collec-
tively, guided by God the Helmsman. But what of we mod-
erns, caught as we are in a sea of our own?

Figure 2. Cuthbert at Sea, in the 12th-c. *Prose Life of Cuthbert,* ex-
tracts from Bede, *Historia Ecclesiastica (History of the English Church
and People)*, British Library MS. Yates Thompson 26, f.26

OVERCOMING THE LIQUID MODERN BLUES

> Producers, both human and non-human, do not so much
> transform the world, impressing their preconceived designs
> upon the material substrate of nature, as play their part from
> within in the world's transformation of itself. Growing into
> the world, the world grows in them. And with this, the ques-
> tion concerning production gives way to another, this time
> about the meaning of history.
>
> Tim Ingold, *Being Alive*

In a world of ecological instability, the storm of our lives tosses us back and forth—literally and figuratively. The ocean is no longer content to remain at a distance, and myriad worlds of water seek to force themselves into our daily lives. The flow of modernity equally abhors a vacuum, seeking to enter and roil within any space of our lives. As Steven Mentz has argued, we are united cross-temporally by our emotional ambiguity towards the oceans of the world. "In physical as well as cultural terms," writes Mentz, "the sea is a very different place from the land. Although our bodies are approximately two-thirds water, water is a hostile element that threatens human life.[33] As Mentz has recently argued, our current thinking is failing us and we must adapt to a new, 'post-sustainable' oceanscape, a notion that resonates in the figurative ocean of life.[34] Disaster is inevitable, our response open to interpretation. To quote Jeffrey Cohen and Lowell Duckert in their recent introduction to a themed issue of *postmedieval* on the topic of ecomaterialism, "catastrophes precede and follow any stability; failures inevitably arrive. In such moments of perturbation we behold the web of interrelationships that constitutes and sustains our own worldedness. Cataclysms inevitably shatter such ecological meshworks, but failure is an invitation to dwell more carefully, fashion more capacious perspectives, and *do better*."[35]

As our institutions crumble, our cultures intermingle, our grasp on the triumphant anthropocentrism of the Enlightenment fades, what must we do?[36] How do we *do better*? Alcuin and Hugh sought order in the intricacies of spiritual edifice, and yet even our minds flow away before us, leading to destinations tantalising and terrible. Flow is both our greatest distraction, and our most vibrant opportunity. We

[33] Steve Mentz, "Toward a Blue Cultural Studies: The Sea, Maritime Culture, and Early Modern English Literature," *Literature Compass* 6 (2009): 1001–1002 [997–1013].

[34] Steven Mentz, "After Sustainability," *PMLA* 127.3 (2012): 586–592.

[35] Jeffrey Jerome Cohen, and Lowell Duckert, "Howl," *postmedieval: a journal of medieval cultural studies* 4.1 (2013): 4 [1–5].

[36] In an interesting passage of relevance to humanists, an article in *The Baffler* describes the now-vanished dream of tertiary education as "the four-year luxury cruise that will transport us gently across the gulf of class." As the ship of university goes down, academics in particular must learn to swim anew, for good or ill. See Thomas Frank, "Academy Fight Song," *The Baffler* 23 (2013): http://thebaffler. com/past/academy_fight_song.

are embroiled in a fraught fluid socio-political ecology, in what Zygmunt Bauman has famously termed liquid modernity, a world in which the "new piety" is to believe that "it is preferable to slip, shift or float than to know, stop or stay" as Adam Phillips put it.[37] And yet, we need not be lost: it is possible to follow flow to new and wondrous destinations.[38] Tim Ingold eloquently captures this spirit when he argues that the "ocean of materiality" humanity inhabits "is not the bland homogeneity of different shades of matter but a flux in which materials of the most diverse kinds, through processes of admixture and distillation, of coagulation and dispersal, and of evaporation and precipitation, undergo continual generation and transformation."[39] We can learn, we can adapt, and as Ingold claims, we can follow the inhuman resonances of becoming to our advantage:

> . . . haecceities [sets of relations] are not *what* we perceive, since in the world of fluid space there are no objects of perception. They are rather what we perceive *in*. In short, to perceive the environment is not to take stock of its contents but to *follow what is going on*, tracing the paths of the world's becoming, wherever they may lead us.[40]

Flow is both our greatest distraction, and our most vibrant

[37] Adam Phillips, *On Flirtation: Psychoanalytic Essays on the Uncommitted Life* (London: Harvard University Press, 1994), 124.

[38] There are many sociological texts in addition to the already mentioned corpus of Zygmunt Bauman and the fluid relations of Ingold advocating a fluid negotiation. For two of the most seminal, see the republished copy of John Urry, "Mobile Sociology," *The British Journal of Sociology* 61, Supplement 1 (2010): 347–366, and Manuel Castells, *The Informational City: Information Technology, Economic Restructuring, and the Urban Regional Process* (London: Wiley-Blackwell, 1989).

[39] Tim Ingold, *Being Alive: Essays on Movement, Knowledge, and Description* (London: Routledge, 2011), 24.

[40] Note that a haecceity is a "thisness," from the Latin *haecceitas*, but that Ingold has used the word to explicitly refer to relationality based on a Deleuzo-Guattarian formulation taken from Gilles Deleuze and Féliz Guattari, *A Thousand Plateaus: Capitalism and Schizophrenia*, trans. Brian Massumi (Minneapolis: University of Minnesota Press, 1987). See Ingold, "Point, Line and Counterpoint," 154.

opportunity. Alcuin was forced to leave his cell and engage with the world, and yet the memory of his sweet abode (his *habitatio dulcis*) remained. The heart of our fluid world, its *oikos*, lies at the center of endless motion, and yet we must cultivate the little space of slow time, the contemplative heart, within us. Perhaps, in imitation of our medieval forebears, we can invest ourselves in cultivating our observer position in the heart of ecology so that we too might seek that which is worthy of lasting affective engagement. Our response? Fluid. If, as Michel Serres has suggested, "order exists not through resistance to change, but through the temporary maintenance of structured change," then the secret to finding our *oikos* must also be a structured form of change.[41] The alternative is a reactive, uncritical panic and paralysis which is, to my mind, the very antithesis of humanistic thought. Zygmunt Bauman characterizes this problem aptly:

> Fear prompts us to take defensive action. When it is taken, defensive action gives immediacy and tangibility to fear. It is our responses that recast the sombre premonitions as daily reality, making the world flesh. . . . Among the mechanisms vying to approximate to the dream model of *perpetuum mobile*, the self-reproduction of the tangle of fear and fear-inspired actions comes closest to claiming pride of place.[42]

To succumb to this fear, to incorporate a model of endless headlong flight into daily life, is to mistake precaution for action. The ennui that results from this practice over the long term, a symptom of liquid modernity living, is the 'liquid modern blues' of the subtitle above. Tim Ingold has suggested that our new space is one of flows, and yet we can cultivate a pluripotency of adaptive responses to unforeseen changes. We can follow the paths of becoming rather than struggling for stasis.[43] This is not an answer to the effects of a fluid ecology of the inhuman, but it is a start in the cultivation of our own internal practices, a modern equivalent to

---

[41] Michel Serres, *The Birth Of Physics*, trans. Jack Hawkes (Manchester: Clinamen, 2000), xi.

[42] Zygmunt Bauman, *Liquid Times: Living in an Age of Uncertainty* (Cambridge: Polity Press, 2007), 9.

[43] See Ingold, "Point, Line, and Counterpoint," 141–155.

the medieval navigation of the *mare mundi*. Unlike medieval people, our ontological conceits do not allow for the deferral of stability beyond time. We must overcome fear and seek opportunity in ecology.

Just as Hugh of Saint-Victor counselled the cultivation of skill and discipline in the face of the liquid medieval, so too may we use our self-apprehension to grow in the world as it grows in us. Just as Timothy Morton advocated the embracing of ecology, even the ugly, the abject and the dangerous, so too must we embrace this danger. We are surrounded by strange strangers, as Morton puts it, eternally strangers and eternally strange by virtue of their strangeness.[44] If this danger is ever present and its causality is endlessly distributed across an inhuman web, how do we find the space to grow? If we humanists are slow recording devices invested in receptiveness to the sound of things, as Eileen Joy has suggested in *Animal, Vegetable, Mineral*, the first volume in this series, then how – and this is an open question to the reader – do we engage while making space for contemplation?[45] We, like a gestation process, need time and nourishment to come to our potential. How are we to grow when the past hurtles into the future with remorseless abandon? The answer, inspired by the medieval wrangling described above, is not to fortify our minds and lives. We can synthesize, we can build and we can strengthen, but we must allow ourselves the flexibility to flow with the forces that work about and within us.

[44] See Morton, *The Ecological Thought*. The notion of the strange stranger appears *passim* in the book, but is introduced in chapter two (59–97).

[45] Eileen A. Joy, "You are Here: A Manifesto," in Jeffrey J. Cohen, ed., *Animal, Vegetable, Mineral: Ethics and Objects* (Washington, DC: Oliphaunt Books, 2012), 169 [153–172].

INHUMAN

Ian Bogost

The Beast. That's what my friend Cliff Bleszinski calls his new Lamborghini Aventador, a four-hundred thousand dollar, scissor-doored, twelve-cylinder, one and a half-ton mass of Italian bravado that accelerates from 0–60 in less than three seconds. The name is apt, and not just because of its prowess on the road or racetrack. Lamborghini tradition dictates that its models take their names from Spanish fighting bulls. Aventador's predecessor Murciélago takes its name from such a bull, named after a bat, which survived twenty-four impalements in an 1879 fight against Rafael Molina Sánchez, a matador known as "El Lagartijo," the Lizard. The bull survived, and the Lizard spared its life. Legend says that Murciélago was presented to the breeder Don Antonio Miura (another Lamborghini namesake), where it served as stud for generations of uncastrated bovine beasts.

For each pair of sword strokes wrought by the Lizard, two cylinders would later grow from Murciélago's corpse. Among its bovine progeny, some might have made their way into the stables of Don Celestino Cuadri Vides, whose sons bred Aventador a century later. For his courage in a 1993 corrida in Zaragoza, Aventador was awarded the Trofeo de la Peña La Madroñera, the most prestigious award of courage awarded in the Plaza de Toros de la Misericordia. An aventador is a flame-fan, a bellows, like the stroking pistons that pressurize and ignite fuel and air in its automobile namesake. The bull, the bat, the lizard, the fire, the engine, the sports car. The Beast. In history and myth and fiction, the beast is not just the animal, but the animal *as opposed to the human*. The beast is dangerous, cruel, violent, *inhuman*.

But as Murciélago and Aventador remind us, things inhuman also have the capacity to overheat and flip into their opposites. When pushed to its limits, Aventador the bull's wild ferocity becomes valiant courage. When the flames in its cylinders are fanned too far, Aventador the automobile's rev limiter staunches them into levelheadedness. The overheated bull becomes more human in its virtue; the overheated auto becomes more human in its incapacity. Both are *less* than human insofar as some of their powers exceed us enough to threaten cruelty and barbarism. Yet they are *more* than human insofar as those very powers of excess can push them back into the realm of civility. Such a contradiction is possible because inhumanism is two-faced. Lacking the human qualities of compassion, that is, being *less* than human on the one hand, but on the other hand possessing greater prowess than humans, being *more* than human. The fighting bull and the sports car are brutal and merciless in their strength and power and speed, because such properties so far exceed human ability. The inhuman is both subhuman and superhuman all at once. It names a friction point between these two poles, where the metaphorical gears of things grind as they mesh.

Once you start looking closely at mentions of things "inhuman," you see this rhythmic two-faced version of it more than the standard derogatory, degrading version. In 1965, Jack Kirby and Stan Lee introduced a group of superheroes called the Inhumans in the *Fantastic Four* comic book. Hailing from Attilan, the Inhumans share the familiar comic trope of genetic mutation: they were conceived by the alien Kree people as a powerful, mutant race of soldiers for use against an alien empire called the Skrull. But the Kree abandoned their efforts after a prophecy foretold the likely fall of their empire at the hands of the mutants they had themselves fashioned. Some Inhumans are inspired by Greek mythology and philosophy—Medusa, who can animate and control her long, red hair to move, lift, and whip her hair;

Gorgon, whose bull's legs can stomp to make shockwaves; Triton, who can breathe underwater and withstand deep sea pressure; Crystal, who can manipulate the Empedoclean elements of earth, air, fire, and water. Others have more secular inspirations: Karnak the philosopher, who can divine weakness; Maximus the telepath; and Black Bolt, the leader of the Inhumans, whose "quasi-sonic scream" does such damage that the hero must avoid uttering all sound.

Like the X-men, who have been made more familiar to audiences unfamiliar with comics thanks to a recent series of successful films, the Inhumans form a secluded society, where they perfect their ability to develop powers through mutation. But of course, those powers also cause deformities and perversions. The connection to Greek myth evokes ἁμαρτία, the tragic flaw, the unwitting mistake that prevents the hero from realizing an objective and instead being saddled with its opposite. Oedipus's hastiness, Othello's jealousy, and so on.

But the mutations of the Inhumans (or the X-men) are not really the same as a tragic flaw. It's not error that leads them to a final and definitive unraveling, but a constant, ongoing state of affairs. The inhumanity of the Inhumans isn't their downfall, but their daily life, their mundane, ordinary practice. And the difference between a tragic flaw and an ongoing rift is repetition, a repetition that changes the nature of the separation between in- and -human. While ἁμαρτία negates the purported features of a hero, inhumanity oscillates them at high-speed, until they settle into the rhythmic hum. Inhumanity is an engine running well, rather than one ground to a halt when a wrench is thrown in it. But like an engine, inhumanity burns and explodes, it wages war with itself on the inside. While Oedipus and Othello are ignorant of and later undone by their flaws, Black Bolt knows his power all too well, for it mediates his every moment.

THE FRICTION POINT

Inhumanity throbs with friction. But today, we strive to reduce or remove this friction rather than to embrace it. Even the Lamborghini's gears can no longer be ground, for the driver need not bother coupling them. Instead, a semi-automatic clutchless transmission effects computer-controlled gear changes in one twentieth of a second. The sensation of feeling the collar disengage and reengage with the action of the gear selector is replaced by the unseen operation of electronic sensors and pneumatic actuators, themselves hidden by button-press.

But things are most themselves (and therefore most interesting) when they don't quite line up, when the gears grind a bit rather than coupling smoothly. When it comes to matters inhuman, the mistake we make most is failing to focus on and amplify the friction point between the familiar and the alien, to replace them with explanation or ignorance. Flat ontology is the premise, suggested by Manuel Delanda and refined by Levi Bryant and others, that being is non-hierarchical.[1] As I have glossed it before, *all things equally exist, yet they do not exist equally.*[2] I have suggested further revising flat ontology to remove not only its third but also its second dimension, compressing the plane into the point. This *tiny ontology*, as I've been calling it, is a singularity, like a black hole. It possesses two sides of two corresponding sizes: one infinitely dense and small—the fact and uniqueness of being as such or of a particular being—and the other infinitely abundant and large—the possibilities its capacities represent when actuated. Those familiar with Graham Harman's metaphysics might translate these two sides into his concepts of the *real* and the *sensual*, the fact of withdrawal serving as the fulcrum, like the narrow throat between the two ampules of an hourglass.[3]

When it comes to the inhuman, we tend to focus on the state of *being* sub- or superhuman rather than on the writhing, shifting friction point between them—the meeting the real and the sensual. Consider an example from medieval literature. In Marie de France's twelfth century *lai* "Bisclavret," the titular lord splits his time between being a respected knight and a feral werewolf. His only salvation from his bestial state come from the human adornments that allow him to transit between the forest and village, between the animal and human worlds. But his lady betrays him by stealing these vestments, and the knight is trapped in lupine form. When the king discovers the wolf, Bisclavret humbles

---

[1] Manuel DeLanda, *Intensive Science & Virtual Philosophy* (London: Continuum, 2005), 58; Levi Bryant, *The Democracy of Objects* (Ann Arbor: Open Humanities Press/MPublishing, 2011), 19–20.

[2] Ian Bogost, *Alien Phenomenology, or What It's Like to Be a Thing* (Minneapolis: University of Minnesota Press, 2011), 11.

[3] For the most concise explanation, see Graham Harman, *The Quadruple Object* (Hants, UK: Zero Books, 2011), 20–50.

himself, and the courtiers conclude that some humanity must reside in him, even though they do not yet know that the wolf is "really" a man. Later in court, Bisclavret attacks the new lord of his former lady, and then the lady herself, severing her nose from her face. The lady confesses, and the knight's human form is restored, while the lady becomes a new type of disfigured beast: not a wolf with its prominent snout but a living human with death's face: a noseless skull. Marie de France thus presciently anticipates modern pop culture by offering us knights, werewolves, and zombies in the same story.

There's been much debate over the noun become a proper name *bisclavret*, particularly since Marie's text suggests that there is some distinction between the ordinary werewolf and the *bisclavret*, a word that is etymologically mysterious:

> "Dame, jeo devienc bisclavret:
> En cele grant forest me met,
> Al plus espés de la gaudine,
> S'i vif de preie e de ravine."[4]

If you stop to think about it, the remarkable thing about being a respected knight for half the week and a silvan wolf for the other is not so much being a wolf or a knight, but of becoming *either* a wolf or a knight: in the transformation itself. And despite the dominant interpretation of the *lai*, Bisclavret's wife does not abscond with her lord's *humanity*, but rather with the hinge between his humanity and his animality. Even though "bisclavret" is generally considered to refer to the man in his lupine state, the term is better seen as a means to draw our attention to the *transformation* between man and beast, rather than to the wolf individually. Take this passage as a starting point:

> "kar si jes eüsse perduz
> e de ceo feusse aparceüz,
> bisclavret sereie a tuz jurs;
> jamés n'avreie mes sucurs" (73–76)[5]

---

[4] Lines 63–66. Roughly translated: "My lady, I become a Bisclavret [werewolf]. I enter the forest and live on prey and on roots within the thick of the woods." Old French cited from Marie de France, *Lais*, ed. Alfred Ewert (London: Bristol Classics Press, 1995).

[5] Roughly translated: "for if I ever were to lose [my vestments], or

The baron warns his lady that if he were to lose his vestments, he would be a bisclavret forever, without any comfort. There's no doubt that the literal meaning of "bisclavret" as "werewolf" is foregrounded here; if the knight cannot transform from man to beast and back again, then he would be stuck forever as werewolf. But something stranger is at work in the baron's attitude.

The bisclavretine state is not merely a state, nor merely a synonym for werewolf. In fact, Marie de France uses the Norman word "garwaf" to gloss the Breton term "bisclavret." But even more so, Bisclavret also names the lai and the baron, he is not just a bisclavret but also, and perhaps foremost, Bisclavret.[6] Under this interpretation, which can stand beside the conventional one thanks to the ambiguity of bisclavret's signified, the baron not only beseeches his wife that he should remain werewolf, but that he would not be able to exercise the relief associated therewith. It's tempting to believe that the baron would simply prefer to be human and cast aside the curse of part-time werewolfhood, but the remainder of the lai suggests that he embraces his fate. Relief is not so much a matter of returning to human state, but of *being able* to do so, of exercising the friction point between human and werewolf. The lady did not steal Bisclavret's humanity when she conspired to abscond with his clothing and thereby to preserve him in lupine form, nor did she fix him in a bestial state, as proved by the wolf's gentle disposition to the king who later orchestrates his return. Rather, she stole the transformation itself, and this loss is greater than that of merely being wolf.

It makes sense: the werewolf is not a man who is also a wolf, nor a wolf who is really a man, but a being who transforms between human and lupine states. Otherwise a werewolf would simply mean a wolf, or else a man, but not both. It's rather an obvious matter, isn't it? The feature distinctive to the werewolf is its ability, often involuntary, to shift between states. We tend to focus on the wolf form, probably because it is far easier to perceive the wolf than to see the

---

even be seen casting them off, I would walk as bisclavret for all my days, and never would I have relief."

[6] In particular, Leslie Sconduto has made this argument, citing the capitalized name and the use of the definite article as evidence. See Sconduto's book *Metamorphoses of the Werewolf: A Literary Study from Antiquity through the Renaissance* (Jefferson: McFarland, 2008), 40.

moment of transformation. Indeed, that moment of transformation is most often hidden or obscured in fictional accounts of werewolves, particularly in television and film where the transformation between human and wolf, wolf and human both involves requires special effects or computer graphics to represent visually, and implies or requires nudity to show directly. Even in situations when the budgets and scruples are lined up to support such requirements—such as in the HBO series *True Blood*—the werewolf's transformation is still condensed, abridged into a singular moment occupying but a few frames. Over time, we have involuntarily trained ourselves to ignore these messy moments of transformation in favor of the stable states on either side.

We can generalize this lesson. "Inhuman" isn't a characteristic of humans or creatures, but one of the many names for the meeting point between things, of the passageways between entities' withdrawn, real being and their sensual encounter with others. It is a membrane rather than a property. The friction point, not where smooth Deleuzean gel oozes between cogs, but where gears grind, where sparks fly. Such friction points are common, but they are hard to see if we focus on the human or humanoid actors that so frequently carry them out.

Take my Lamborghini-driving friend Cliff Bleszinski again. He is known for designing *Gears of War*, a dark, gruesome shooter with hulking, square-jawed protagonists named Marcus Fenix and Dom Santiago who wield huge guns with chainsaw-bayonets. It risks drawing games' usual rejoinder, that of doing little more satisfying the brutish power fantasy of adolescent boys. But underneath its dudebro exterior, *Gears of War* is built around the mechanics of cover, of moving between areas of exposure to slowly, deliberately advance upon the game's bestial Locust Horde enemy. It is not so much a shooter as a how-do-I-get-to-shooter, a game whose subject is exposure more than it is combat. Not *being* exposed, but the moment between safety and hazard. Like the gestalt of an optical illusion or the shapeshift of a werewolf, this topic is a thing no less than a chainsaw or a lizard or a fire is a thing. It's just hard to see because we tend not to look for it. We look for processes in beings rather than holding that all processes are beings too.

Can a wolf yield as if it were a knight? Can a bull have courage as if it were a man? Can an automobile ignite a driver as if it he were an inferno? These are metaphors, but they are also real.

Lamborghini named the finish color that coats Cliff's vehicle Arancio Borealis, an Italo-latinate pidgin phrase that renders into English as the prosaic "northern orange." To his credit, Cliff uses the correct vulgar translation: asshole orange. That's not a boast; it's an admission, a kind of dude-bro name for the same inhumanism Marie de France calls bisclavret. It's an admission that the coupling between driver and Lamborghini is not primarily about accelerating from 0–60 in 2.9 seconds. Rather, it's about transitioning between the mundane and the extraordinary, finding that membrane between the sub- and the superhuman. Opening or closing a scissor door, or stowing a load of groceries in the tiny boot, this is the meaning of Lamborghini ownership, like lancing Marcus Fenix over a crumbled wall is the meaning of *Gears of War*, like Bisclavret hiding his clothes in the hollow of a rock, like willing courage out of a fighting bull just by naming it "courage."

THE ALIEN INVASION ALREADY HAPPENED

Still, superheroes and supercars are overly dramatic examples. The encounters between more mundane objects are always just as feral as Murciélago the bull or Aventador the coupe. Normally we don't notice them. Usually, it takes something exceptional, like a medieval werewolf or an expensive sports car to expose these chasms between things. Instead, we might do better to look past the spectacle of the sports car and the supernatural beast.

As Black Bolt and his Attilans prove, there's a strong link between inhumanity and alienness. Aliens are the flipside of the inhuman, the deep-space black-hole source of inhumanity. We usually understand the alien either in a political or a cosmological sense: a terrestrial alien is a foreigner from another country, and an extraterrestrial alien is a foreigner from another planet. Even when used philosophically to refer to otherness more generally, aliennness is assumed to be a human-legible intersubjectivity. Whether from another nation or another galaxy, the other is someone we can recognize as enough like ourselves to warrant identification, just as an inhuman act is one we can recognize as contra-human versus a-human. The former suggests the intention to act against human interest, while the latter merely suggests having a state of no particular concern for or about humans.

But why should we be so selective, so self-centered as to think that aliens are those beings whose intelligence we might recognize as intelligence, or that inhumanity is a force mustered against humanity? As the philosopoher Nicholas Rescher has observed, a true alien might not even have an intelligence akin to our intelligence. Rather than wondering if alien beings exist in the cosmos, let's assume that they are all around us, everywhere, at all scales: not just dogs and penguins and magnolia trees, but also cornbread and polyester and the city of Orlando and sidewalks and nectarines. I started asking one particular question about their inhumanity, a question I have previously given the name *alien phenomenology*: what do objects experience? What is it like to be a thing?

I came to this question by accident, in much the same way that Bisclavret must have been made garwaf, or that the Inhumans decocted their powers out of the Terrigen Mist. Years ago now, I learned how to program the Atari Video Computer System, the 1977 console that made home videogame play popular. My colleague Nick Montfort and I were working on a book about the relationship between the hardware design of the Atari and the creative practices its designers and programmers invented in those early days of the videogame.[7] To understand this strange device, we had to seek out its interstices, to find its friction points. In order to produce television graphics and sound on the cheap, Atari designed a custom chip called the Television Interface Adapter (TIA). It was capable of rendering five moving objects. For better or worse, thanks to the Atari movement and collision became the grammar of videogames. The TIA made bizarre demands: instead of preparing a screen's worth of television picture all at once, the programmer had to alter data the TIA transmitted in tandem with the scanline-by-scanline movement of the television's electron beam. Programming the Atari feels more like plowing a field than like painting a picture.

As critics and engineers, Nick and I were interested in the Atari's role in human creativity and culture: how computer hardware influenced game design and aesthetics. You can see the effects of the TIA's line-by-line logic in Atari games: in the rows of targets in *Air-Sea Battle* or the horizontal bars of horizon in *Barnstorming*. Methodically, we pointed out these couplings between machine and expression in the

---

[7] Nick Montfort and Ian Bogost, *Racing the Beam: The Atari Video Computer System* (Cambridge: M.I.T. Press, 2009).

popular games of the era, from *Combat* to *Adventure* to *Pit-fall!* to *Yars' Revenge*. How, why, and by what accident these games were made. The Atari was made by people in order to entertain other people, and in that sense it's just a machine, a machine for humans, an artifact of humanism, even. But a machine and its components are also something more, something alive, almost. I couldn't help but feel enchanted by the system's parts as much as its output. I found myself asking, what is it like to be an Atari, or a Television Interface Adapter, or a cathode ray tube television? These couplings and relations enter the domain of inhumanism, one possible name for the powerful and unseen couplings between things.

How do we train ourselves to see them? We'd need to change our attention, to see a world in which we nurture more than just our own progress or profit, but one that also rubs up against the weird fate of everything else. This is not simply a world of "interconnection," of anonymous assem-blage, of anything-goes, distinction-free philosophies of murk. To acknowledge and attend to anything is precisely the opposite of attending to *everything*, for everything is just a stand-in for nothing.

When we talk about being "brought up," we usually refer to culturing a way of relating to other living beings—human beings of course, but also animals, and perhaps even the natural environment. This process involves ethical impera-tives, directives about what to believe about and how to act upon the world. We give comparatively little thought to our *aesthetic* rearing, the matter of how we orient toward things (and how things orient toward one another) rather than what we do to them.

I suppose it makes sense that the Lamborghini or the werewolf are necessary piques. They rupture the ordinary world. The werewolf is a less likely sight in ordinary life, so consider the supercar as an instructive real-world example instead. You pull up to a light or into a parking space to find the Lamborghini or Porsche or Maserati or even the Tesla. It stands out; sometimes via asshole orange pomposity, some-times via simple peculiarity. Those of us in possession of the memory of childhood—or even adult—fascinations with supercars might make appeals to desire: for power, for wealth, for speed, for possession. But when confronted with the reality of such vehicles, those fantasies quickly melt into far less dramatic realities. The surprisingly wide wheelbase of the Ferrari Testarossa that, inexplicably, is driving down the side street behind your high school or workplace. The unfamiliar ornament or emblem that makes you realize, actually, I'm not even sure of the logo or motto or symbol for this object of purported fantasy. Somehow, even just seeing an absurdly expensive automobile in the flesh has the power to siphon out a steady stream of pedestrian relations that get covered over on glossy magazines. The impracticality of twenty-inch tires against the under-maintained asphalt of your city's roads; the surely-outlandish insurance premiums; and even then, the impossibility of parking without worry, either risking a nick or a key, or becoming that dick who parks out in the corner of the lot, across three spaces, the asshole earning his paint's namesake.

But we need not focus on such superhuman objects to tease out their ordinariness. If anything is truly exceptional, perhaps it is unexceptionalism, for the mundane surrounds us so completely that we fail to notice it. The rain's condensation on the windowpanes, or the cut of a wool skirt against the cold, blue dawn, or the tapioca pearl against the walls of the doublewide boba straw—these meetings are just as lurid.

We have humanism and posthumanism in philosophy and criticism already. What would an inhumanism look like? It wouldn't mean an abandonment of humanity, nor an endorsement of violence or reproach against humanity. Rather, it would invert the pigments of our usual ontological attention, like a film negative reflects areas of high exposure with high colorization instead of low. If Bisclavret teaches us that the friction points between man and wolf are where the action's at, action we've been missing while attending obsessively with the man-wolf and the wolf-man on either side, then an inversion of this overt humanism would focus on the interstices of such entities, the friction-filled couplings between them. Or, to use another analogy, inhumanism is akin to filling in all the space in a structure with plaster, letting it harden, and breaking apart the resulting mold in order to observe what takes place in the spaces otherwise unoccupied with our attention.

The inhuman isn't against us so much as it is alien to us; it recedes interminably even as it surrounds us completely. It is not hidden in the darkness of the outer cosmos or in the deep-sea shelf but in plain sight, everywhere, in everything. We are wanderers in an exotic world of utterly incomprehensible objects, that nevertheless we might try to comprehend. You and me, all of us, just another thing. Inhumanism is not posthuman nor anti-human. It's far less interested in humanity than such terms call for. It names an attention to the infinitely deep and numerous chasms between things, the tiny points where the real meets the sensual, over and over. It's the domesticated study of aliens and beasts, the alien as *intra-terrestrial* rather than extra-terrestrial, the beast as commodity varmint rather than monster. Like aliens, beasts are just names for things. The beast in the cabinet, the beast on the supermarket endcap, the beast on the powerlines and flowering off the grasses, the beasts between the covers of this book. Tupperware lids and videogame consoles as much as fighting bulls and electron-focusing superheroes.

Perhaps some day we will pore over them with the attention and seriousness we have hoarded for poetry or for identity politics. That would be a real inhumanism indeed. I wonder if we are brave enough to face it, to face the parking blocks and the screen phosphor like the matador faces the bull, like the werewolf faces the forest.

51978822R00093

Made in the USA
Lexington, KY
12 May 2016